Authoritative, accessible, and specific—this guide is an invaluable resource.

—Gretchen Rubin, Author, *The Happiness Project*

Karen Leland has one of the best grasps on branding I've seen. *Ultimate Guide to Pinterest for Business* is more than just a book on using Pinterest for marketing, it's a handbook for anyone who wants to understand how to approach branding and social media in today's complex online world.

—Olivia Fox Cabane, Author, *The Charisma Myth: How Anyone Can Master the Art and Science of Personal Magnetism*

Karen is the behind-the-scenes secret for the success of many small business brands. Her take on Pinterest makes this a fascinating book with a roadmap on how to use this popular platform to increase community engagement, brand visibility, and sales.

—Susan Harrow, Author, *Sell Yourself Without Selling Your Soul*

Leland shows you exactly how to use this wildly popular tool to pull in more customers and boost our brand's visibility and credibility.

—Kare Anderson, Author, *Moving From Me to We*, "Quotable and Connected" Columnist, *Forbes* and *Huffington Post*

If you haven't figured out how to make Pinterest work to build your brand, business or platform, Karen Leland's book gives you the details you need to get results without wasting your time. Pinterest is a force to be reckoned with when you know what to do and how to do it, and Karen does both.

—Mike Koenigs, CEO, Instant Customer

Can you make money using Pinterest? Absolutely! Karen Leland's new book shows you the exact steps to master the art of relationship marketing on Pinterest. Read this well-written, comprehensive book, and you'll be attracting and converting leads into paying customers in no time!

—Mari Smith, Social Media Thought Leader, Author, *The New Relationship Marketing*, Co-author, *Facebook Marketing: An Hour A Day*

Every small business should read this book—not only because it will show you exactly how to use Pinterest to promote your business, but for the marketing and branding lessons Karen Leland has managed to weave throughout the book. Make Pinterest work as hard as you DO!

–Berny Dohrmann, Founder, CEO Space, Bestselling Author,
Redemption the Cooperation Revolution

Ultimate Guide to Pinterest for Business provides the reader with a step-by-step approach and a clear path for maximizing communication in their business or profession. Karen's in-depth knowledge of social media, marketing, and branding are a bonus for anyone wanting to integrate Pinterest into their marketing mix.

—Michelle Patterson, Executive Director, California Women's Conference

Karen Leland's *Ultimate Guide to Pinterest for Business* is a gem! She has provided the must-have, must-read playbook for pinning in business. I've learned so many ideas, details and strategies that will impact and improve the Pinterest portion of my business and life.

—Susan RoAne, Author, *How To Work a Room* and *The Secrets of Savvy Networking*

WOW. This book is AMAZING! If you're ready to learn everything you need to know about successfully using Pinterest, then read and absorb the strategies in this brilliant book by Karen Leland!

—James Malinchak, The World's #1 Big Money Speaker® Trainer & Coach featured on ABC's hit TV show, "Secret Millionaire," Founder,
www.BigMoneySpeaker.com

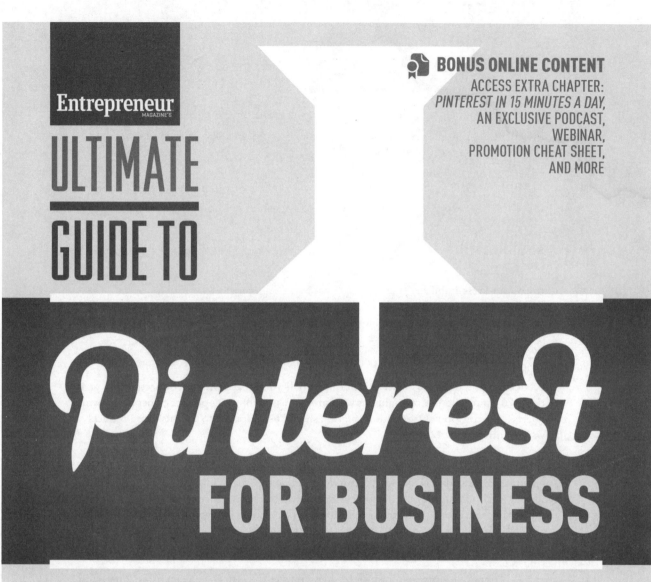

Entrepreneur MAGAZINE'S

ULTIMATE
GUIDE TO

Pinterest
FOR BUSINESS

- Master the A-Z Guide on Using Pinterest In Your Profession
- Curate Content and Build Boards That **Convert Customers to Buyers**
- Create a Savvy Pinning Strategy to Drive Traffic, Build Your Brand, and Boost Business

Entrepreneur
PRESS®

KAREN LELAND

Entrepreneur Press, Publisher
Cover Design: Andrew Welyczko
Production and Composition: Eliot House Productions

This publication is designed to provide accurate and authoritative information in regard to the subject matter covered. It is sold with the understanding that the publisher is not engaged in rendering legal, accounting or other professional services. If legal advice or other expert assistance is required, the services of a competent professional person should be sought.

Library of Congress Cataloging-in-Publication Data
Leland, Karen.
      Ultimate guide to Pinterest for business: master the A-to-Z guide on using Pinerest in your profession, curate content and build boards that convert customers to buyers, create a savvy pinning strategy to drive traffic, build your brand, and boost business / by Karen Leland.
      p. cm.
      ISBN-13: 978-1-59918-508-8 (alk. paper)
      ISBN-10: 1-59918-508-3 (alk. paper)
      1. Internet marketing—Social aspects. 2. Pinterest. 3. Web sites—Design. 4. Branding (Marketing) I. Title.
      HF5415.1265.L455 2013
      658.8'72—dc2   2012050781

Printed in the United States of America

17 16 15 14   10 9 8 7 6 5 4 3 2

Dedications

To my first grandson, Oscar Leland. Welcome to the world. May the changes brought about by technology in your lifetime enhance your creativity and liberate your spirit.

And to Jon Leland, Oscar's grandpa and my husband of the past 20 years. The road has not always been easy, but it's been a journey. I would not be the person I am today without you. All my love.

Contents

Acknowledgments

As the saying goes, "It takes a village," and that's as true for writing a book as it is for raising a child. This is the eighth book I've had the privilege to write over the past 20 years, and it's clearer to me than ever that without the love, support, and encouragement of my friends, family, clients, and support team, neither this book nor any other could happen. Special thanks to:

Jeff Herman, my literary agent and the one who sent me the email inquiry while I was visiting Vietnam to see if I'd be interested in writing a book on Pinterest. He convinced me that, despite the tight timeline for turnaround, it would be worth the effort. He was right, and I'm glad I took the plunge.

Caitlin Oliver, my research assistant, without whom I never could have achieved said timeline (see above for details). Her quick turnaround, courteous emails, can-do attitude, and research abilities helped make this book possible.

Nell McPherson. Where would any of us be without a good copyeditor? Fast, effective, and responsive, you catch the mistakes I miss. Thanks for keeping the grammatical gremlins at bay.

Andrew Simon Leland, my stepson, father of Oscar, and a star writer and editor. When I called desperate for a research assistant, he found me Caitlin within the week. Eternal gratitude.

Susan Harrow, for always being in my corner when I doubt myself, cheering me on when things get tough, lifting me up when I'm down, and inspiring me with her own excellence, humanity, and work ethic to be the best that I can be.

Anne Christine Strugnell, my good friend and fellow writer. Many a day Anne Christine sat at one end of my dining room table working on her personal essays for such magazines as *More* and *Self*, while I sat at the other end working on this book. Her mere presence was a productivity enhancer and a true pleasure.

Sami Cohen, for his deep wisdom, guidance through a rough patch, and for really seeing who I was through it all.

My fabulous group of girlfriends, who sustained me with love, understanding, and chocolate during the writing of this book—Kim Bromley, Liza Ingrasci, Dianne Morrison, Lynette Sheppard, Theresa Souers, Dr. Alyse Danis, Sheila Vasan Singla, Anne Christine Strugnell, Susan Harrow, and Randy Roberts—you are all the wind beneath my wings and I can't even conceive of what my life would be like without you.

Jon Leland, my husband, tech guru, and go-to guy whenever some technical point about Pinterest had me cocking my head to one side like a confused cocker spaniel. Thanks for saving me in so many ways more times than I can count, in life and in business.

My clients at Sterling Marketing Group. Most of my workdays are spent having interesting conversations with the smart people I am lucky enough to call my clients. They do me the honor of allowing me to contribute to their success and in return have taught me an immeasurable amount about what it takes to practice branding, marketing, and running a business in a wholehearted way. I thank them from the bottom of my heart.

Jillian McTigue, Rose Ellen D'Angelo, Ron Young, and Karen Billipp from Entrepreneur Press. Flexible, supportive, cooperative, nice to deal with. Can you really ask for more from your publisher?

What Is Pinterest, and Why Should You Care?

As someone who does marketing and branding strategy and implementation, it's my job to stay on top of the latest and greatest in the world of would-be life-altering internet bells and whistles. Ironically, however, the last thing I wanted to do was learn yet another social media tool—that promised to transform my online life.

But day after day, my husband, Jon, would flash his iPad in front of my face and tease me with all the new, cool photos he was pinning on Pinterest. Besides, I was scheduled to give a talk on social media for book promotion at an upcoming International Book Publishers Association conference in San Francisco. So I threw my hands up in surrender and let Pinterest have its way with me—and I'm glad I did.

WHAT EXACTLY IS PINTEREST?

Pinterest is a lifestyle brand that allows you to create a visual, online pinboard, organized around topics of your choice by category. For example: I'm a certified chocoholic, so I started a Pinterest board on dark chocolates I love—featuring photos of said delicacies accompanied by mouthwatering descriptions.

WHO IS USING PINTEREST, AND HOW ARE THEY USING IT?

At the time of this writing, Pinterest has more than 10 million users and is the fastest growing social media site in history. Beyond that, the various and sundry stats that are shaping Pinterest include:

- A review of Google Display Network Ad Planner, a free tool for building online media plans, shows that 72 percent of Pinterest users are female, and 66 percent of those are age 35 or older.
- A Pew Internet & American Life Project survey of U.S. adults found that nearly 20 percent of women using the internet are on Pinterest.
- According to Experian, a global information services company, the average amount of time visitors spend surfing the Pinterest site is an hour.

If those statistics don't make a small-business mind sit up and take notice, nothing will. But in a space crowded with would-be Facebooks and Twitters, how did this social media star get its start?

A BRIEF HISTORY OF PINTEREST

Ben Silbermann was on track to follow in his parents' footsteps as a doctor when he heard the call of the online world. Silbermann left premed in his junior year of college, began regularly perusing blogs such as TechCrunch, and persuaded Google to hire him to work in design.

Inspired by the big-idea thinking at Google, Silbermann had no lack of product ideas, but did lack the engineering background to execute them. Enter his college pal Paul Sciarra, whom he teamed up with to make iPhone apps—all of which failed.

In March 2010, however, the two launched Pinterest and, for the first nine months, had only 10,000 users—5,000 of whom Silbermann had personally contacted to get the site started and keep it going.

A little over a year later (June 2011), Pinterest was garnering media attention and rapidly growing its customer base, and, by August 16, 2011, *Time* magazine had named it one of the 50 Best Websites of 2011.

According to Hitwise data, by December 2011, the site had become one of the top 10 largest social network services, with 11 million total visits per week, driving more referral traffic to retailers than LinkedIn, YouTube, and Google+.

In 2012, TechCrunch named it the Best New Startup of 2011, and in March 2012, it became the third-largest social network in the U.S. Co-founder Paul Sciarra left his position at Pinterest in April 2012, for a consulting job as entrepreneur in residence at Andreessen Horowitz, but Silbermann remains as CEO.

Fast-forward to today, and Pinterest has become a Silicon Valley darling because of its rapid user growth. In 2012, the company raised $100 million in a financing round that valued the startup at $1.5 billion.

WHAT THIS BOOK CAN DO FOR YOU

Things change fast on the web, and a relatively new player like Pinterest is guaranteed to go through growing pains and organic adjustments in its first few years of existence.

So while this book is not meant to be a blow-by-blow tutorial of how to take every action possible on Pinterest, it does aim to provide both beginning users and seasoned veterans with the ability to find their specific area of interest "at a glance." This book is organized to take you through a logical and sober process of building a Pinterest account. It uses step-by-step how-tos, sidebars, examples, case studies, expert interviews, and tip sheets to show you how, from setup to strategy, you can use Pinterest for your promotional, branding, and marketing objectives.

Keep in mind that if you don't find a tip or technique you are looking for in one place, it most likely is living in another part of the book. So I encourage you to make good use of the index at the back to find what you are looking for. To this end, the book explores:

- The ins and outs of signing up and getting started on Pinterest
- Building boards that get noticed, drive traffic, and convert fans into customers
- Creating your Pinterest community through high-engagement activities, contests, social media outreach, and smart pinning strategies
- Specific marketing applications of Pinterest to small businesses, from architecture firms to theater companies
- Strategies for becoming a power Pinterest user and creating an enthusiastic following
- Best practices for pins that promote, including image optimization, consistent branding, social media integration, and high-value content
- Pinterest etiquette
- A plan to implement all the "to-do" items you generate out of this book

THE RISE OF THE VISUAL WEB

Finally, no self-respecting preface would be complete without providing an appropriate context for the book that follows. So here it is:

Great business brands are about telling compelling, congruent stories, and Pinterest is at its core about storytelling in pictures. Where this social media big dog goes from here is anyone's guess, but part of Pinterest's power is in its stronghold in the game of the visual web.

Let's face it: People love pictures. We spend hours uploading images onto Facebook, scrolling through YouTube videos, and surfing the web for snapshots of things we want to do, be, or have.

Pinterest has tapped into this visceral love of visuals, and no small business, entrepreneur, or corporation can afford to miss the boat on bringing what they do beyond words and into images.

By following the best practices outlined in this book, becoming inspired by the case studies and stories told, and taking the marketing strategies offered to heart, you can make the most of Pinterest to expand your business and brand's success—one pin at a time.

Thanks for reading, and happy pinning.

—Karen Leland, Sterling Marketing Group,
www.karenleland.com, Tiburon, California

For additional free tips, ideas, ebooks, webinars, and other goodies on Pinterest and other social media and marketing topics, please visit www.karenleland.com.

Chapter 1

On Your Mark, Get Set, Join

Every January 1st, I sit down at my dining room table, glue sticks, scissors, and stacks of magazines at the ready. For several hours I hunker down to cut and paste images and words onto an 8.5-by-11-inch piece of white card stock. The final product is a personal vision board for the year—a place where all my goals, hopes, plans, and purposes are represented on one neat, tidy piece of paper.

Pinterest is the digital version of this cutting and pasting process—but much less messy since no glue sticks enter the picture. As with any analog inspiration board, your own creativity is the driving force behind what you curate, but with Pinterest you have the added advantage of being able to put up both images and videos.

Whether you're reading this book because you have heard that Pinterest is the hottest thing since sliced bread and you know you need to be on it or you're already a member and looking to achieve peak performance, it's the aim of this book to help you use Pinterest to its maximum capability.

This first chapter will provide you with all the basic technical ins and outs you need to get going on Pinterest. Consider it the crash-course primer and necessary evil of learning all the boring stuff so you can move on to actively using Pinterest as part of your marketing mix. So, as Julie

Andrews sang with such gusto in the movie musical *The Sound of Music*, "Let's start at the very beginning."

WHAT EXACTLY IS A PIN?

In its simplest terms, when you land on a Pinterest page, if you look below the menu and browsing bar, you will see a set of neatly laid-out rows and columns of images. Each one of these images is a pin. Because Pinterest adjusts the layout based on browser window size, you may see up to ten columns of pins at a time, but no fewer than three (see Figure 1–1).

As you scroll down, the columns of images will grow longer as the Pinterest feed fetches the older pins from people you follow. Images nearer to the top of your page are the newest pins from your feed.

FIGURE 1–1. A Sample Pin Board from *Entrepreneur* Magazine
(http://pinterest.com/entmagazine/)

KNOW THY LINGO

If you moved to France, you would at least learn a few basic phrases so you could get by, *oui*? Taking a few minutes to familiarize yourself with them now will help you get the most out of reading this book and using Pinterest.

KNOW THY LINGO, CONTINUED

- *Pin*. An image added to Pinterest from a website or an image on your computer.

- *Board, aka Pinboard*. A board is a set of pins created around a specific topic. You can add as many pins to a board as you desire. Boards can be public (seen by everyone) or private (viewing by invitation only). However, at the time of this writing, Pinterest has limited each account to only three private or secret boards.

- *Pinning*. The act of placing content (images, video) onto a particular board.

- *Pinner*. The person doing the pinning, the user.

- *Repin*. Adding an image you find while browsing Pinterest to your own board. A repin maintains the source link of the image no matter how many times it's repinned.

- *Like*. Liking a pin adds the image to your profile's Likes section; the image does not get added to one of your boards, as it does when you repin an image.

- *Following*. "Following" someone means you'll see that person's pins shown to you in real time on Pinterest. If he/she creates a new board, you'll automatically follow the new board as well. You can follow individual boards if you're only interested in seeing pins being added to specific boards. You can unfollow other people or boards at any time, and they will not be notified.

- *Follower*. Someone who is following your Pinterest boards or one or more of your individual boards.

- *Mention*. A way to mention a fellow pinner by typing the @ symbol immediately followed by his/her name in a pin description. You can also mention a user in a comment. Mentioning a fellow pinner brings you to their attention and is one way to reach out and connect with other users. For more details, see Chapter 10, "Engage with the Pinterest Community."

- *Hashtag*. A way to tag a term using the # symbol that makes it findable by other users searching for that same word or phrase. For example, if you pin an infographic on five ways to organize an office, you might want to hashtag it as #timemanagement. This way, when a user puts the phrase "timemanagement" into Pinterest search, all the pins with that hashtag come up—including yours.

WHAT INFORMATION DOES A PIN CONTAIN?

Pins can be composed of images, videos, slideshows, or audio. But they are more than that. Although images are the driving force behind Pinterest, a pin's visuals should be accompanied by:

1. A description of the pin (500 characters or less)
2. The pinner's name (and the original pinner, if the image has been repinned)
3. The name of the board that the pin is housed under.

Directly below the text of the pin description are a few metrics:

- Number of likes (if any)
- Number of repins (if any)

If people have commented on the pin, comments will be listed below the pinner's name. We will go into more detail on pins and pinning in later chapters, but for now, this info is the bottom line you need to know before jumping in and joining.

SIGN ME UP

For the first few years of its life, Pinterest was invitation-only, and you had to either submit a request through the Pinterest website or receive an invitation from a friend who was already on Pinterest. In the summer of 2012, the party went public and anyone could sign up—no invitation required. There are two ways to join Pinterest. One is as an individual, and one is as a business or brand.

Join Pinterest as an Individual

To play, just go to pinterest.com and find the big, red, can't-be-missed "Join Pinterest" button at the top of the page.

Click the link, and you are whisked away to a new page that gives you the option of creating your account via Facebook, Twitter, or your email address. Click the logo of the service you wish to connect through.

One thing to consider: If you have a Facebook account, you may want to choose this option as your initial setup, since it will enable you to view all of your Facebook friends who are on Pinterest immediately.

If you decide to go the sign-up-through-your-other-social-media route, either the Facebook or Twitter login page will pop up once you have made your selection. Enter the email address and password you would use to sign into that particular site, and then click the "Log In" or "Sign In" button. In the case of Facebook, a screen will pop up with a green "Go to App" button in the upper right-hand corner. Click through to the "Create Pinterest Account" page.

If you choose the third option of using your email to join, click the email link located below the Facebook and Twitter sign-up button. Clicking that link takes you straight to the page where you enter a Pinterest username, your email address, a password, and your first and last name. You can also upload your Pinterest profile picture on this page. Click "Create Account" to submit your information and, presto, you are a part of Pinterest.

Create Your Pinterest Account

Regardless of which way you choose to connect (Facebook, Twitter, or email), you will be asked to choose a username and password for your Pinterest account. A few things to keep in mind include:

- The URL for your Pinterest profile will be based on your username, so make sure it's consistent with your desired brand. For example, my username is karenleland; hence, my Pinterest URL is https://pinterest.com/karenleland/. It's important to note that if you choose Facebook to set up your Pinterest account, your username gets automatically created for you. If you use Twitter, you have to choose a username at sign-up.
- A username can only be three to 15 characters long with no spaces, symbols, or punctuation marks, so if the username you want is already taken, try adding numbers to your name or choosing an alternative that still would have you be easily found by your personal or business name.

When you're done filling out the form, click the "Create Account" button at the bottom of the page and Pinterest will then present you with a wide array of boards—by category—and ask you to pick five to follow as a way to get started. After choosing your first five boards, hit the "Next" button at the top of the page and you will be asked to create your first board. Once you have created a board, you will be ready to rock and roll. Go to the drop-down menu under your name and click on "Settings," then proceed to fill out your Pinterest profile. For details see Chapter 2, "Create a Pinterest Profile That Rocks."

Sign Up as a Business/Brand or Convert an Existing Account

When Pinterest first began, no option existed for formally distinguishing between a business or brand and a person. Today you can sign up as a business or convert an existing personal account to a business account. Depending on what your primary goal is for Pinterest, you may want to join as a business or brand, not as an individual. Some people also choose to have two Pinterest accounts—one personal, one company. But beware: Having two Pinterest accounts means double the amount of work.

To convert your existing account or to get started for the very first time, simply go to http://business.pinterest.com/ or click on the "For Business" tab under the "About" drop-down menu. From there, click either the red "Convert your existing account" button or select the "Join as business" link just below it.

You will then be directed to a page where you fill out your business profile. For specifics see Chapter 2, "Create a Pinterest Profile That Rocks."

A TOUR OF THE PINTEREST INTERFACE

Before you delve into the wide world of pinning, it's worth your while to take some time and familiarize yourself with the Pinterest interface. A basic understanding of the site's simple, clean layout will make navigating easy (see Figure 1–2).

The "Search" Box

At the top of the Pinterest homepage is the menu bar. At the far left is the "Search" box. Use this box to find pins, boards, and people within the site. Type what you are looking for into the "Search" box, and click the magnifying glass.

The Pinterest Logo

To the right of the "Search" box is the Pinterest name logo. This logo is a link. Any time you want to return to the Pinterest feed/homepage, just click the logo, which is always present in the top center of the screen.

The "Add+" Button

At the far right of the menu bar is the "Add+" button. Click it and a small screen will pop up providing you with an option to add a pin, upload a pin, or create a new board.

The "About" Drop-Down Menu

Next to the "Add+" button is the "About" drop-down menu; where you can find an endless amount of information about Pinterest. Hover your cursor over "About," and you will see a list of clickable options including:

FIGURE 1–2. Pinterest Interface

Help

The "Help" section of the site contains information on a wide variety of Pinterest processes, including "Pinning 101," which explains all the basic functions of Pinterest and provides profile and account setting instructions as well as guidance on pinning and repinning, commenting, managing boards, and much more. If you ever get stuck, this is the first place (other than this book) to look for answers.

The "Pin It" Button

Directly underneath the "Help" section is a tutorial about how to install the "Pin It" button on your web browser for easy pinning. The "Pin It" button allows you to instantly pin content when surfing the internet.

For Business

By adding "For Businesses" as a drop-down choice in the "About" Tab on the homepage, Pinterest has made a point of providing businesses with ideas for how to enhance their performance on the site. Clicking on this link takes you to a new page. Immediately under the "Convert Your Existing Account" and "Join As A Business" links are four categories for exploration.

- Tell your story
- Build a community
- Send traffic your way
- Learn and grow

Clicking on each of these categories leads to a page featuring ideas and examples of how businesses and brands are using Pinterest in the most effective ways.

See how others are doing it

Directly underneath the four categories for exploration is a section titled "See how others are doing it." This section highlights five case studies of companies that have made significant marketing inroads with Pinterest.

Find useful tools and brand guidelines

Pinterest's goal is to make it easier for businesses to integrate various Pinterest tools into their websites, and this section contains buttons and widgets to help boost your Pinterest traffic. These include:

- The Pin It Button
- The Follow Button
- Add a Board Widget
- Logos, Trademarks, and Marketing Guidelines

Careers and Team

Do you love Pinterest so much you want to work for them? The "Careers" link provides information about working for the company, and the "Team" link just below it lets you see all the people who run Pinterest.

Blog

The Pinterest blog contains the latest news and updates about the site, the company, and its services. The blog also features Pinteresting trends, site tips, and "Pinterviews" (interviews with fellow pinners).

Terms of Service

As with any social media site, Pinterest requires that you agree to certain conditions. This section shows (in great detail) exactly what you signed up for, including Pinterest's limited liability and how you can, and can't, use the content contained on the site.

Privacy Policy

How does Pinterest collect your information? What information do they collect, and how do they use it? How can you protect your privacy while using Pinterest? Answers to all of these questions are contained in this section.

Copyright and Trademark

These two sections contain the official Pinterest policy regarding intellectual property. If you feel that someone on Pinterest has violated your personal copyright or trademark, you can follow a link to register a complaint.

Your Pinterest Account

Next to "About" will be another drop-down menu marked by your name and a thumbnail of your profile picture. Hover your mouse over your name to see these clickable options:

Invite Friends

You can use this section to invite friends to Pinterest by entering their email addresses and typing a personal note in the box provided. Click the red "Send Invites" button when done, and you're on your way to building your Pinterest community.

Find Friends

If you want to invite to Pinterest people whom you are already connected with via Facebook, email, Yahoo!, or Gmail, this section makes it easy by allowing you to pull up a list of your current contacts.

Boards

Clicking on this link brings up a screen of all your current boards. It also contains some basic metrics listed at the top of the page including:

- Total boards you have created
- Total pins you have pinned
- Total pins you have "Liked"
- Number of followers you have
- Number of pinners you follow

Pins

This section presents all of your individual pins, from all of your boards, all at once. The information at the top of the page is the same as with the "Boards" link, and the link below Pins contains the "Likes" tab, where all the pins you have "Liked" come up on the screen at one time.

Settings

If things change down the road and you need to edit the information in your profile, or even deactivate your account, this is the place where you can easily update your email, password, profile description, location, website, image, and Facebook and Twitter logins.

Logout

You can log out of Pinterest at any time, but remember that if you want to use the "Pin It" button while surfing the internet, you have to remain logged in, even if you don't have the Pinterest window open in your browser at the time.

THE BROWSING BASICS

Now that you know how to navigate through Pinterest, the last tutorial before sending you on your way to pin to your heart's content is an overview of how browsing works on the site. On the home Pinterest page, just below the main menu bar, is a second mini-menu with five items, beginning with "Following." The five items are:

1. *Following.* By default, whenever you log into Pinterest, you will visually see images from the people you follow on Pinterest and the "Following" tab will be highlighted.

2. *Categories.* To the right of "Following" is the "Categories" menu, which displays the 32 different Pinterest categories available—everything from Architecture to Outdoors, Humor to Gardening. There is also an "Other" category for pins that don't fit neatly into one of the named buckets.

3. *Everything.* Located in the middle of the mini-menu, clicking on this link opens the page to a mix-and-match jumble of all the most recent pins on the site, from fashion to food.

4. *Popular.* Moving along, further to the right is the "Popular" link, which features the current most popular content on Pinterest.

5. *Gifts.* The final link in the mini-menu is "Gifts," which is a drop-down menu of items specifically available for purchase and organized by price range from $1 to $500+. Simply clicking on the "Gifts" link without selecting a price range from the drop-down menu will take you straight to a page displaying gift pins, regardless of price.

Now that you've got the lay of the Pinterest land, it's time to take the plunge and craft a profile that establishes you on the site.

Create a Pinterest Profile That Rocks

In the previous chapter, you learned how to join Pinterest as either an individual or a business/brand. Once connected, your next step is to set up your account profile—and here's where you have an opportunity to create a killer first impression.

If you're a serious entrepreneur, hot-shot marketer, or just plain smart, you will take the time to maximize your Pinterest profile to its fullest. The more the people who check out your pins know about you, the stronger your personal and business brand will be.

For individuals, before you begin to enter your autobiographical information, Pinterest will ask you to follow five boards that share your same interests. Not to worry; you can always unfollow them later when you have time to step back and apply some strategic thinking to the types of boards you want to create, including the names you give them. In Chapter 4, you will find step-by-step instructions on setting up, naming, and designing your boards.

For businesses and brands, you will be taken directly into the profile setup as part of joining, without having to choose starting boards. While the process for creating a profile is similar for businesses and individuals, there are some slight variations. But since there are some overlaps, read through the information for creating each for the useful tips that apply to both.

CREATING AN INDIVIDUAL PROFILE

Once you have chosen a few starter boards, you will need to locate the settings file, under your name, and complete the profile process. Profile elements include:

Email

Not to worry; this isn't shown on your public profile.

Email Preferences

By default, Pinterest is set up to notify you right, left, and center about all the great new happenings in the world of all things pin, such as news updates and a summary of weekly activity. Pinterest will also email you when:

- One of your pins gets liked
- One of your pins receives a comment
- One of your pins is repinned
- One of your group pinboards receives a new pin
- A new user decides to follow you

If all this sounds like just too much of an inbox influx of pinning information, your notifications are the place in your profile to set limits. By going through each of the various options, you can change your email settings to decide when you do and do not want Pinterest to let you know when one of the above actions is taken.

First and Last Name

This is a different field than your username on Pinterest and should reflect your real name, or the name of your business, if your account is being set up for your business.

Username

As discussed earlier, if you created your Pinterest account via Facebook, your username was automatically generated for you. If you signed up via Twitter, you provided a username. In either case, your username is critical because it becomes the URL upon which your Pinterest account is based.

Gender

Now, if this one seems obvious, Pinterest, in all their political correctness, has provided the option of "unspecified" as a gender choice. So if you just don't feel like being pinned down (no pun intended), you're free to stay uncommitted.

About

Pinterest only gives you a brief 200 characters to describe yourself or your business in this section, so make them count. They are text-only and can't be changed into bold or italics, just plain old letters. Since these are the details that someone sees when they visit your profile page, aim for information that lets the viewer get an at-a-glance look at who you are, what you offer, and why they should care. You may want to consider including your basic elevator speech about what you do; your book, business, or product name; what you are passionate about pinning; and your website address. By the way, it won't be a live link, so skip the "http://" and just go with "www."

Keep in mind that to strengthen your brand, you should maintain a consistent message across all your social media platforms. This means that a similar description should show up on Pinterest, Twitter, Facebook, LinkedIn, and any other places on the internet where you publicly declare your brand.

Location

One advantage to adding your location to your profile is that potential customers looking for a local resource will be able to see that you are geographically desirable. If for some reason you would rather remain a gypsy, just leave this section blank.

Website

Pinterest only allows you to list one website URL, so if you have several websites, think carefully about which one you place here. In general, I recommend to my clients that they use their main website. You can always go back later and easily change this by editing your profile. By the way, unlike in your "About" section, this website URL is a live link represented by the world symbol under your profile pic, which visitors can click through to your site.

Profile Photo

If you are one of those people who think that forgoing a profile photo is an OK option—it's not. By some accounts, social media profiles with photographs are seven times more likely to be viewed than those without. When you first sign up for Pinterest, it will pull a profile image from whichever social network (Facebook or Twitter) you connected with at startup. However, you can change that image at any time via three methods:

Upload an Image

This allows you to instantly browse your computer and find the image file you want to upload as your profile picture. The exact size of your Pinterest profile picture is 160 by

160 pixels. Stretching or shrinking to fit will automatically resize square images that are larger or smaller than 160 by 160 pixels. Rectangular images are centered, resized, and cropped, possibly leaving you with a profile picture that is less than optimal. For this reason, the ideal image is a square photo around 200 by 200 pixels in size.

Refresh from Facebook

If you have chosen to integrate your Facebook with your Pinterest account, you can instantly update your profile photo to match the image being used on your Facebook account. Just click "update," and your profile is automatically changed. Remember to hit the "Save Profile" button at the end before exiting.

Refresh from Twitter

Opting to also connect your Twitter account to Pinterest works in the same way as the Facebook button. You can change your current profile image to match the one you are using on Twitter with one click. Again, save before exiting to have the change take hold.

FACEBOOK AND TWITTER ACCOUNTS

Even though Pinterest no longer requires you to sign up by linking to your Facebook or Twitter account, once you are in, you can adjust your profile to link as you like. However, before taking this step, consider a few things:

By turning on the "Publish Activity To Facebook Timeline" button in the settings, you are creating another form of engagement with your tribe. If you're worried about bombarding your friends with nonstop images, don't be. Pinterest publishes your pins as a group, not one at a time.

If you want to Tweet your pins, switching the "Login with Twitter" setting to "On" allows you to automatically send any new pin you create to your tweet stream by simply checking the Twitter box that appears when you create a new pin.

To Hide or Not to Hide?

Most people want their Pinterest boards to be as public and accessible as possible for marketing and branding purposes. But if you want to hide your Pinterest account from the search engines, you can do so in your profile settings, via an on/off button at the bottom part of the profile page, just above the "Delete Account" button. When you start your account, the default setting is "off," which I recommend you keep. For most people, being found via a search engine is a plus. However, if you really want to keep your Pinterest activity private, go into the profile and adjust to turn "on" the privacy setting.

If you're thinking that this all seems to be much ado about nothing, consider this: The first impression you make on a Pinterest user who stops by your boards for a peek can determine your long-term online relationship. Whether they become a fan who regularly repins your work, a loyal follower who clicks through to your website and converts into a buyer, or a one-time drop-by can rest on the strength of your personal profile.

CREATING A BUSINESS PROFILE

As part of signing up for a business/brand account, you will be automatically directed to the business profile page. If you already have a personal account and are converting to a business account, some information will automatically fill in from your personal profile, but you can modify or edit it to reflect changes. The profile questions include:

Business Type

Whether you are new to Pinterest or converting an account, you will be asked to choose a business type from nine categories.

- Professional (attorney, blogger, artist, etc.)
- Public Figure (actor, musician, politician, etc.)
- Media (magazine, newspaper, channel, etc.)
- Brand (Lululemon, Burger King, Marvel, etc.)
- Retailer (Nordstrom, Pier 1, etc.)
- Online Marketplace (eBay, Amazon, etc.)
- Local Business (tattoo shop, specialty grocery, etc.)
- Institution/Nonprofit (World Wildlife Fund, Amnesty International, etc.)
- Other

While your business or brand may fit under more than one category, other users will find you by type, so pick the most relevant to your brand. You can always change it later.

Contact Name

The name of the contact person for the Pinterest account. This could be you or whoever manages the social media for your business.

Email Address

The email address of the account's contact person.

Business Name

This is the way you will appear on Pinterest, so you can either use the Pinterest username from your current account or choose a new name for your business or brand.

About

If you are converting an account, your previous bio will be automatically filled in and you can make changes or leave as is. If this is a new account, you will need to fill out this section.

Terms of Service

To finalize your business account, you must indicate that you have read and agree to the "Terms of Service" at the bottom of the page. The conditions aren't radically different from a personal Pinterest account; the only real difference is the acknowledgment that businesses may use Pinterest for commercial activity, which, while previously permitted, is now explicitly OK. Please note that Pinterest still reserves the right to remove any content that violates their "Acceptable Use" policy such as pornography or spam.

Once you have provided all the information, go to the bottom of the page, and click "Convert" or "Create Account" to continue with your setup.

Get Started with Your New Business Account

Now that you have officially declared yourself a business with Pinterest, you will be taken to a screen that provides you with four options for next actions:

1. Verify Your Website

Following these instructions ensures that your full website URL shows up in your profile.

2. Start Pinning

This takes you through the steps to install the Pin It Bookmarklet so you can easily pin images from a website to one of your boards.

3. Drive Traffic Back

Provides a "Pin It" button you can add to your website that makes it easy for people to pin from your website to Pinterest.

4. Grow Your Audience

A "Follow" button you can add to your website that invites visitors to click through to your account and follow you on Pinterest.

SIX WAYS TO STAR IN YOUR PROFILE PIC

Let's face it: We have all shaken our heads in horror at the unfortunate profile photo of someone doing tequila shooters in their bathrobe. Don't let this be you. The profile picture you pick may seem like a simple thing, but it has an immediate and weighty impact on a visitor's first impression of your Pinterest page. If you are going with a personal photo rather than one of your business logo, here are six things to keep in mind when deciding which image to upload as your Pinterest profile photo.

1. *Axe the avatars*. Unless the very essence of your brand is a cartoon character you have created and whose face is what you show the social media world, from LinkedIn to Google+, skip the avatar, please, and let us see the real you.

2. *Please face the camera*. While sexy looks over the shoulder and sideways glimpses of your fabulous face might work great for a fashion shoot, they are the opposite of what you want in a Pinterest profile picture. The best option is to post a photo where you are looking straight into the camera, full face forward.

3. *Lose the accessories*. The purpose of your profile photo is to give a visitor a quick hint about who you are as a person. Depending on the message you are trying to send, wearing sunglasses; holding Fido, your surfboard, or a glass of anything alcoholic; or even having another person in the photo with you can give the wrong message. Think carefully about the communication you are crafting with who and what is with you as you take the shot.

4. *Keep it current*. If you start showing up to client meetings and hear, "Wow, you look different than you do in your profile," call a photographer today. You may really love how you look in that headshot from the last decade, but, unless you've found the fountain of youth, it's out of date. A good rule of thumb is to have your photo updated every two to three years. This covers changes in hairstyles, fashion, and—sigh—aging.

5. *Go light on the airbrushing*. If you're 50 years old, and have NO wrinkles on your face, you just look like you are trying too hard. Just remember, people

SIX WAYS TO STAR IN YOUR PROFILE PIC, CONTINUED

do business with people they like and trust. If you show up in meet space and don't look reasonably like you do in your online photo, your credibility is compromised—even if unconsciously—in the other person's mind.

6. *Stay consistent.* If you have a professional social media profile pic you are already using for your other sites, such as LinkedIn, Twitter, Facebook, etc., consider using this same one for Pinterest. A consistent image across all these platforms can be a visual personal brand strengthener.

UPDATE YOUR PROFILE ANYTIME

Regardless of whether you signed up for an individual or business/brand account, you can always go back and update or edit any information in your profile. So just in case you decide to go from undecided to female or male in the gender category—no worries. Simply sign in to your Pinterest account, then click the "Edit Profile" button under your profile picture and above your boards. You can update any of the information you originally entered, including adding a different website and even changing your username. Beware that a change in username may cause you to lose followers you have built up. Remember when you are finished editing your profile to hit "Save Profile" at the bottom of the page to put the changes into effect (see Figure 2–1 on page 19).

By this point you are probably itching to get pinning, but hang tight. Before we set you loose to create killer boards that will brand your business to the next level, you need to step back and strategize based on what you want to achieve with Pinterest and how it fits into your overall marketing mix.

Email Address	kleland@scgtraining.com **Email Settings**
Password	**Change Password**
Language	English ▼
Gender	○ Male ⊙ Female ○ Unspecified

PROFILE INFO (shown publicly)

First Name	Karen
Last Name	Leland
Username	karenleland http://pinterest.com/username
Image	**Upload an Image** **Refresh from Facebook** **Refresh from Twitter**
About	Best selling author/President of Sterling Marketing Group/ Enthusiastic about branding, marketing & content development/Writes the Modern Marketing Blog at 12 characters remaining
Location	San Francisco, CA e.g. Palo Alto, CA
Website	http://www.karenleland.com **Verify Website**

FIGURE 2–1. Basic Profile Information Can Be Changed At Any Time

Strategize First, Pin Second

The beauty of Pinterest is that, aside from the unacceptable content (porn, illegal activity, etc.) specified in their user agreement, you can pin almost anything your heart desires on the boards you create.

However, randomly pinning pictures without thinking through a strategy for how you want to use the site won't net you the best branding or marketing results—or even the greatest degree of personal satisfaction.

Before you launch into heavy pin-and-promote mode, think it through and even consider writing up a one- or two-page Pinterest Business Plan that answers the following three critical questions.

1. Is your Pinterest for personal or business branding?
2. Who is your target market?
3. What are your marketing goals?

IS YOUR PINTEREST MAINLY FOR PERSONAL OR BUSINESS BRANDING?

Since you have the option of creating a Pinterest account as a business/brand or an individual, start by asking yourself what your purpose is in using Pinterest. For most people it usually falls into one of two main categories:

Using Pinterest for Bookmarking Purposes

If your main goal with your Pinterest Boards is to create a holding place for all your good ideas—be they personal or professional—you are probably most interested in using the site as a visual, online bookmarking service. For example:

- You're getting married in June and want a place to put all those floral arrangement ideas you run across.
- You're just crazy about everything and anything puppy dogs and want to be able to view your entire pictorial collection at a glance.
- You're planning a dream trip to the Denver Rodeo and want to keep a log of all the things to do when in town and have a place to post your pics from the trip.
- You're redoing the bathroom and want to have instant access to a visual record of the ideas you might want to consider for the project.
- You're learning to tap dance and want to place the video recordings of your lessons on a board so you can play them back for practice.

What all the above have in common is that these boards are primarily for the pleasure, education, and entertainment of the pinner—not a potential viewer who might see them. In this case, a personal, individual Pinterest account would be a better choice. Nothing wrong with that at all—but as you will see, this is a far cry from using Pinterest for purpose number two.

Making Pinterest Part of Your Social Media Mix

The other focus is on using Pinterest to consciously pin things that relate to your book, business, or product, and that you know your customers, followers, and friends would be interested in seeing. For example:

- You have written a book on time management and create a board featuring your favorite personal productivity tools (that's what I did).
- You have a business that specializes in destination weddings and post pins of the latest, greatest, hottest hotels around the world for getting married.
- You write a popular blog on trout fishing (at last count there were 262,000 based on my Google search) and regularly pin pictures of the places where you have caught great fish—as well as pins featuring the fish themselves.
- You're a marketing consultant and post infographics on recent research you think your audience would find useful.
- You're a tap dance teacher and place videos of you teaching tap to students on a board showing your top-notch techniques at teaching toes how to do the time step.

What all these Pinterest boards have in common is that they are customer centered. In other words, they offer education, entertainment, or information primarily for the pleasure and enlightenment of the viewer—not the pinner. In this case, your best choice would be to opt for a business or brand Pinterest account.

TWO PINTEREST ACCOUNTS

While you can have a combination of both, in most cases you want to think through which one will take precedence and what the real purpose of your Pinterest account is.

Some people get around this dilemma by having two Pinterest accounts, one personal and one professional, each one with a different name—usually the personal is the individual's name and the professional is the name of the company or brand.

By the way, depending on the size of your business and the known strength of your brand, you may want to have your profile pic be your business logo, rather than your face. For larger, most established companies, the logo is often the best way to go.

Smaller businesses, entrepreneurs, and experts such as authors, coaches, and consultants are usually better known as individuals—and therefore are the brand, themselves. In this case, it's best to show a personal face to the Pinterest world to avoid creating customer confusion.

WHO'S YOUR TARGET MARKET?

Depending on which marketing expert you ask, defining your target market is best achieved by looking at either demographics or PsychoDemographics—customer lifestyles, attitudes, and behaviors—or both.

Demographics: Age, Income, and Gender

These represent three of the big dogs in data, and it's worth considering your ideal customer to see if they currently fit within the most common Pinterest user profile.

Age

Think about what role age plays in defining your target market. Do you provide services or products (i.e., beer or baseball caps) that anyone from a 21-year-old to a 91-year-old might buy? If not, what particular age groups do you serve and what are their unique needs?

Income

What level of earning or disposable income do your ideal clients have? The pinner whose business operates at an average sale of $13.99 (vs. the pinner whose smallest sale is $3,999) is going to have to approach what and how they pin in a particular way to meet the monetary considerations of their customer base.

Gender

Does your product or service appeal exclusively to men or women, or is it more inclusive? Men and women respond differently not only to what is offered but to the way things are promoted and displayed.

What the Numbers Say

Now take a look at your answers and compare them with this demographic data according to Google Ad Planner:

- 72 percent of Pinterest users are female
- Average age of Pinterest users is between 25 and 54
- 25 percent of Pinterest users have earned a bachelor's or higher degree
- Majority have a household income of between $25K and $75K

Does your demographic profile fit in with the prototypical Pinterest customer? If so, you may have a match made in online heaven, and it's a good bet you will want to add Pinterest to your marketing mix. If not, you can still maintain a Pinterest presence—just to stay in the game—but it might not warrant putting a lot of time into pinning.

STATISTICS AND DAMNED STATISTICS

A word of warning: Social media statistics—like a love of Cracker Jacks and cotton candy—can change over time. Hence the numbers quoted here are as of publication date and, given Pinterest's relatively new status on the playground, are likely to change. Updated data can be found at several places on the web including: www.experianhitwise.com and www.google.com/adplanner.

PsychoDemographics

Another lens through which to look at your target audience is their lifestyle preferences, personal commitments, and values. Often referred to as psychodemographics, the fine research minds at such companies as Experian Hitwise and Nielsen Prizm research how these distinctions translate into different customer segments.

Understanding the ways in which these factors impact your customers can greatly influence your Pinterest strategy. For example, let's take a look at just one of the segments from Claritas Nielsen Prizm and how they might apply to the Pinterest audience.

The Affluentials

These folks represent close to 23 million Americans with a median income of $66,913. They are typically couples with white-collar jobs and college degrees. Their consumer tastes include home-related items, health foods, computer equipment, and consumer electronics. One of the top followed brands on the web is home design company West Elm (http://pinterest.com/westelm/). With more than 87,000 followers, they do a great job of creating boards aimed at this demographic (see Figure 3–1).

FIGURE 3–1. West Elm Caters to PsychoDemographics with Their Boards

Likewise the magazine *Real Simple* (http://pinterest.com/realsimple/) has more than 192,000 followers and 73 boards that focus on the affluentials' interest in food and home life (see Figure 3–2 on page 26).

Aside from hiring a marketing consultant to create a full profile of your potential customer, here are some of the ways you can identify the PsychoDemographics of your audience:

FIGURE 3–2. *Real Simple*: A Focus on Food and Good Living

- What books and magazines do they typically read?
- What TV shows, or types of TV shows, do they watch?
- Where do they tend to shop (big box retailers, luxury stores, discount marts)?
- What kinds of consumer goods do they tend to buy?
- Where do they spend their disposable income?
- Where do they value spending time (family, work, exercise)?

The bottom line is that you need to look at your customers in total. In addition to traditional demographics, strive to understand your ideal audience's state of mind through PsychoDemographics. Then you can consider the contextual relevance a site like Pinterest will have and strategize accordingly.

UPDATE YOUR AUDIENCE ANALYSIS

In an economy and market that is in a constant state of flux, audience profiles can shift suddenly. If you think that you have done your due diligence by figuring out your ideal client profile five years ago, you're already behind the times. At a minimum, an annual review of your audience will keep you on top of the demographic and Psycho-Demographic changes that can impact your business.

WHAT ARE YOUR MARKETING GOALS?

What is it that you hope to have happen by your participation on Pinterest? As in all social media, you may be looking to achieve a variety of objectives including:

- *Driving traffic to your website.* If your website is the major engine you use to drive sales, an increase in traffic (via Pinterest links) makes pinning a plus for your business.
- *Boosting your brand awareness and building buzz.* Pinterest tends to draw visitors who love to seek and find great things they weren't expecting. That means your boards can get "found" by a whole new audience you don't already have.
- *Increasing sales.* If you sell the type of product that inspires click-here-and-buy behavior, Pinterest can be a great avenue for bumping up your sales numbers in a relatively short period of time.
- *Expanding customer engagement.* Perhaps you see Pinterest as a tool for keeping in touch with your customers. Because it's visually based, your goal might be to practice showing the quirky, fun, funky side of your brand and see what resonates. By the way, if something bombs on a board, you can always dump it.
- *Bonding with your brand fans.* It's worth being on Pinterest just to see which fans, evangelists, and enthusiasts show up on the scene. Creating deeper connections with these folks can often expand awareness about your business at a rapid rate.

In a world where social media tugs at your sleeve daily like the plant in *Little Shop of Horrors* imploring, "Feed me, Seymour," you need a good reason to put time into pinning. By thinking through the answers to the questions posed in this chapter, you can set up a strategy that ensures you win when you pin.

Now that you know where you are going, next up is building the boards and placing the pins that can get you there.

Build Boards That Are On Brand

P interest—as the name aptly indicates—is about pinning images of interest to both you and your customers. The content you feature (your pins) and the way you organize it (your boards) are what define and promote your brand in your audience's eyes. Think of Pinterest as an at-a-glance way to make a first impression about who you are, what you do, and what you care about. The first dimension of this impression is going to be the boards you construct.

14 TYPES OF BUSINESS BOARDS WORTH CREATING

Before you even begin to bring new boards into being, it's a smart strategic move to consider what types of boards would serve you best given your overall Pinterest marketing goals (see Chapter 3 on strategy). In this section we'll explore 14 ideas to consider when building your business boards.

1. Topics That Are of the Strongest Interest to Your Target Audience

In other words, think about boards that would speak to the obvious themes, subjects, areas of interest, and issues that are important to your clients and potential clients. Many, but not all, of your boards will fit into this category since topics of interest are the heart of what you want to focus on to draw visitors to your boards. This can include ideas that aren't spot-on with your business but are related in some way. For example, if you sell high-end stainless steel cookware, it's a safe bet that your visitors are foodies, chefs, or cooks. While a board on party planning might not be directly related to your products, it is tangentially related and would be of interest to your audience.

The Food Network (http://pinterest.com/foodnetwork/), which has more than 52,000 followers, 88 boards, and 1,600 pins, features not only recipes but entertainment and holiday craft ideas as well—both of which are a natural extension for their core audience.

For example, their "Let's Celebrate" board has both a Fourth of July pin for a strawberry rhubarb shortcake and a fruit-tart flag (with a live link to the recipes on the foodnetwork.com site), as well as several red, white, and blue tabletop decorating ideas.

That strategy appears to be working since Pinterest continues to be a top social referrer of traffic to the FoodNetwork.com website. Two chicken recipes on Pinterest alone drove more than 700,000 page views to their sister site, Food.com.

2. Educational Value

What learning can you offer your customers based on your business, book, or product? Boards based on "how to" information do very well on Pinterest. So if you have access to content (video or print) that can educate, inform, teach, or transfer knowledge to your audience, by all means create some boards around it. The nice thing is that as long as the information relates to your business, it doesn't even have to be your original content, so long as you properly credit it.

Video How-To Pins

For example, Flourish Design Studio (http://pinterest.com/weheartdesign/) has a board titled "Wordpress Training" (see Figure 4–1 on page 31) that features a whole series of pinned how-to videos on using WordPress, covering everything from how to create links to embedding video. The kicker is that these videos were not created by Flourish but by a site called wp.tutsplus.com. Flourish has simply pinned them and given proper credit and a link to the content creator's website.

Caution: Copyright is a sensitive issue on Pinterest (and the web in general). Be sure to read the copyright information in Chapter 6.

Image-Based How-To Pins

Video isn't the only way to share how-to content with your clients. Pins based on photographic or infographic "how to" information are just as popular. For example: Net

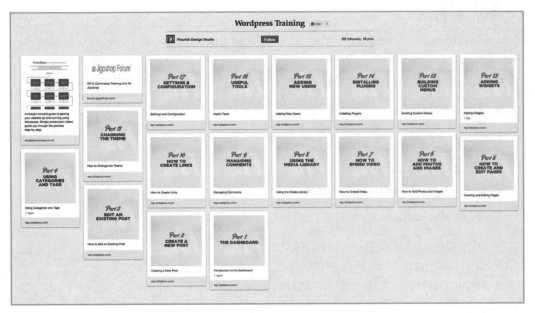

FIGURE 4–1. Video How-To Pins

Positive Impact/Sustainable OBU (http://pinterest.com/sustainableobu/), at Oxford Brookes University, has a board titled "Friday Infographics." Here they offer color-filled charts that educate, teach, and inform on topics such as "How Green is the iPad?" "Cutting Back on Energy Costs," and "Shopping Seasonally."

3. Hobbies, Passions, or Interests That Float Your Boat

Like all other social media sites, an important element of Pinterest is the personal. If you have interests that you feel passionate about, and wouldn't mind sharing them, having a board or two dedicated to them is one way of giving your audience an appropriate peek inside your private world and making you more accessible as an entrepreneur.

4. Feedback for Your Business

Thinking about launching a new service or product? Looking for opinions about how a particular aspect of your business is being received? Want to know what your customers like or don't like about your offers or delivery? Try a virtual focus group by creating a Pinterest board that allows you to test what your target market thinks. Brand managers can post and pay attention to what is getting liked, repinned, and commented on, then pivot as needed.

5. Upcoming Events

If your business is hosting a training, meeting, or upcoming event, create a board that introduces it to your audience. Some ways to promote the event without being overly spammy include pinning information about:

- The speakers
- Workshops and other educational breakouts
- Sponsors
- Location and surrounding area
- Special events within the event

You can also include:

- Blog posts related to the topic of the event
- Special offers for early registration
- Event photos and attendee comments

6. New Products or Services

What are you about to launch that you want to feature? In the same way that you can create buzz for events, you can rev up your audience's anticipation for a new product or service launch by dedicating a board to it. The most effective strategy is to begin the board six weeks to two months in advance. Try pinning information about the features and benefits of your new offering, suggested audiences and uses, and special deals, testimonials, etc. After the release you can post customers' comments, media reviews, and photos of clients using the product or service.

7. FAQ and SAQ Boards

You know the types of questions your clients are always asking . . . and you know the ones they should be asking—the SAQs, or *should ask questions*. Create a board for each type, and use them as a place to send curious clients.

8. Makeover/Before and After Boards

If your business lends itself to visually showcasing before and after images, this board is for you. Businesses that can take the best advantage of this include makeup artists, hairstylists, wardrobe consultants, interior designers, landscape architects, plastic surgeons, cosmetic dentists, and home/office organizers. Even coaches and consultants can use this board by creating pins that showcase impressive outcomes, such as an increase in sales or web traffic, that resulted from their intervention.

9. Holiday Boards

Users are always searching for fun things to pin at the holidays, including things to wear, eat, create, do, and buy. Holiday boards allow you to capture some of this traffic and increase exposure for your brand by pinning relevant and timely images. For example, Chobani (http://pinterest.com/chobani/), a yogurt company, has more than 21,000 followers. Their "Holiday Treats" board features non-yogurt goodies users can make. Pins such as Mummy Meatloaf, Skeleton Brownies, and Shamrock Spinach Quiche all entice users searching for fun holiday foods to click on their profile.

10. Showcase Your Company Culture and Employees

Generate greater customer engagement by giving your clients an inside peak at your business through a board or boards that offer a feel for your company's style, ideas, projects, and commitments. For example Whole Foods (http://pinterest.com/wholefoods/) has a board called Whole Planet Foundation that features pins of projects from around the globe that reinforce the Whole Foods commitment to sustainability, organic farming, and green in general, as well as inspirational sayings that reflect the company's whole living message.

You can also feature photos of your office and employees or even your customers—all with their permission, of course. Acquia, a company that provides cloud-based solutions (http://pinterest.com/acquia), features a board called Our Team Culture that showcases, among other things, the finalists in the company's Ugliest Sweater Contest, team members in London on a business trip, and an Acquia light-up drink-stirrer in action.

BOARDS AND PINS HAVE NO EXPIRATION DATE

Unlike other social media sites, where older posts get pushed down further on the page, pins have no expiration date and can be moved around on a board to be featured at any point in time. So the images of perfectly carved pumpkins that you pinned last Halloween have just as much chance of being picked up and going viral this year.

11. Provide Social Proof

According to Wikipedia, social proof is "a psychological phenomenon where people assume the actions of others in an attempt to reflect correct behavior for a given situation." In other words, if it worked for the Joneses, it should work for me. There are several flavors of boards you can create that will help create social proof.

Feature Your Customers Using Your Brand

Create a board that shows how current customers are using, interacting with, and integrating your product or service into their businesses. One way to do this is to ask people to send you photos of them engaging with your brand.

Profile Your Customers

A board that showcases who your customers are, what they do, and links back to their websites establishes you as credible. If they are willing to provide a testimonial you can include in the pin description, even better. Two cautions: You obviously need to get permission from them to pin their pictures, and you will be letting your competitors in on who you are working with. If both of these are OK, pin away.

Direct Marketing News (http://pinterest.com/directmktgnews/) has a board titled "Our people" (see Figure 4–2) filled with the smiling faces of "The excellent people who have shared insights with Direct Marketing News or been featured in its pages."

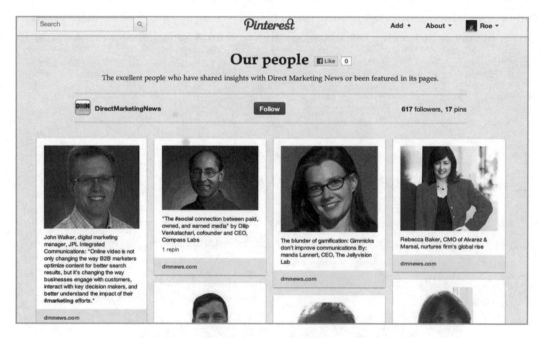

FIGURE 4–2. A Shout-Out to Customers and Clients

Each one comes complete with a description of who the person is and what they have contributed.

12. Your Company's Vision

From startups to Fortune 500, your customers love to be let in on your vision for your business. With Pinterest, you can publicly declare the future you want to create and gather support from your business community. Some of the ways to do this include: images that communicate a feel of where you see your business going, with text that explains the vision, and sayings or quotes from leaders in your company or others expressing company values. You might even consider using Pinterest to create a visual business plan of sorts that shows potential investors, future and current customers, and potential employees where your company specifically sees itself going.

13. Discussion Groups

Like an online forum, a Pinterest discussion group board features a designated topic for discussion and invites other pinners to weigh in with responses in the description box. For example, PediaStaff (see Figure 4–3; http://pinterest.com/pediastaff/) has more than 34,000 followers and 130 boards, several of which are dedicated to discussion

FIGURE 4–3. Host a Discussion Board

groups. The School Psych Discussion Group hosts a board where they encourage school psychologists to talk about ideas or resources they see on Pinterest.

14. Offer Ebooks On Your Expertise

Most companies are built around a particular expertise. A great way to share yours is to pin images that relate to ebooks (or white papers) you have written. The cover of your ebook makes a good image to pin since it makes it crystal clear what the user is looking at. Be sure to link the image to the page on your website where the ebook can be downloaded.

HOW TO CREATE A BOARD

Now that you have an initial list of possible boards, you can create a new board from anywhere within the site by using the main toolbar located at the top of your screen. So if you are browsing another pinner's site and inspiration hits, you can follow the simple instructions to start a new board.

Place your cursor over the "Add+" button, located close to the top right corner of your screen, and click to select it. A new box will pop up, allowing you to choose "Add a Pin," "Upload a Pin," or "Create a Board." Select "Create a Board" to proceed (see Figure 4–4).

From here, you will need to give each board its own individual name. Although this sounds simple, the naming of your boards is a make-it-or-break-it business and branding opportunity.

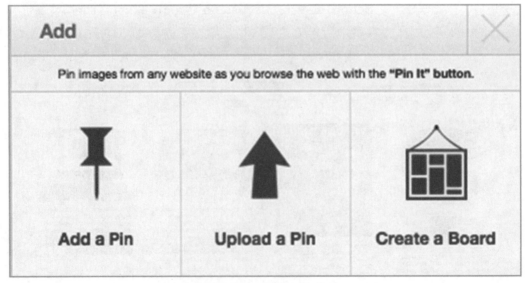

FIGURE 4–4. Add a Board

FIGURE 4–5. "Create a Board" Box

Alternatively, there is a blank "Create a Board" box at the end of the boards on your Pinterest homepage. Click it to open the same dialog box as you see when you create a board using the "Add" feature (see Figure 4–5).

NAMING YOUR BOARDS

Before we dive into the dos and don'ts of board naming, a few things to note. First off, you can have the same name for one of your boards as another pinner has for theirs, since the URL for each board includes a username and hence is unique.

Second, board names have a 180-character limit, so you need to be brief, memorable, and descriptive.

Third, although you can change the title of a board at any point down the road, once established, that board has a dedicated URL associated with it. That means that any links you've previously sent out into the online universe bearing that URL will be

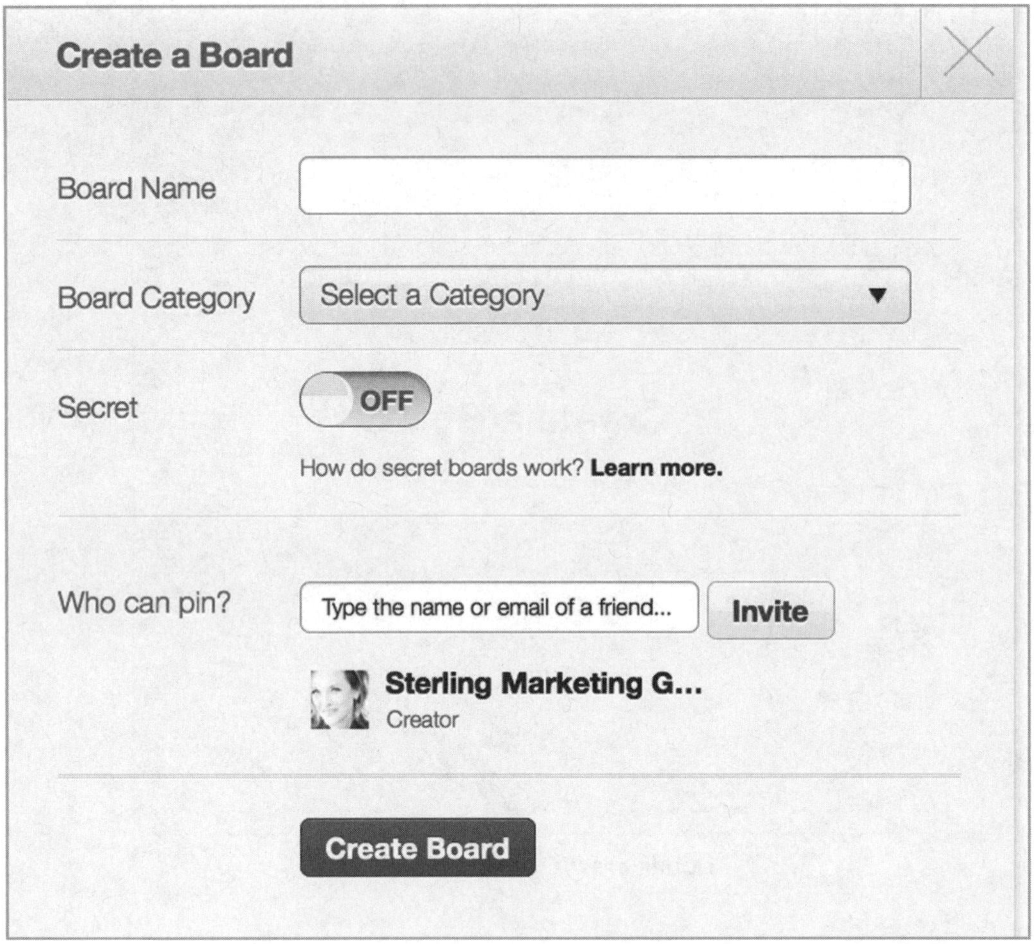

Create a Board   ✕

Board Name   [   ]

Board Category   [Select a Category   ▼]

Secret   [OFF]

How do secret boards work? **Learn more.**

Who can pin?   [Type the name or email of a friend...]   **Invite**

Sterling Marketing G...
Creator

Create Board

FIGURE 4–6. Board Name and Setup

dead as doornails once you change the board's name. For this reason alone, it's best to put some time into thinking about what you are going to call various boards and not rush willy-nilly into board branding (see Figure 4–6). Here are a few good guidelines on crafting winning board monikers.

Be Specific

A common mistake many pinners make is giving their board names that are too broad, vague, and big in scope. For example:

- Things I Love
- Fabulous Finds
- Great things to know about X
- All things X

HIT LIST OF BOARD NAMES

In the course of my research for this book, I ran across a good deal of silly suggestions for using Pinterest, as well as smart and savvy advice. This edited list of creative board names is reprinted with permission from aimClear.com (www.aimclearblog.com)—an Inc. 500 company. Not all these board titles will work for every business or industry, so feel free to borrow and adapt as you like.

Raise Awareness

____ We Admire (could be fundraisers, doctors, writers, lawyers, moms, etc.)

Help Those in Need

Make a Change

Take a Stand Today

Community Power

Words of Wisdom

Inspirational Impacts

Amazing Stories from You

Create a Community

Tell Your Story

Show the Impact

Watch Us in Action (videos)

Eventful!

Why We Are Here

Be Prepared

Meet Our Team/Join Our Team

Through the Years (history of your organization)

____ Like a Pro (weld, eat, shop, travel, speak, write, golf, etc.)

The Wonders of ____

DIY____

Safety First

Industries We Service

Watch Us ____

Before & Afters

On the Job With Us

Success Stories & Testimonials

Trusty Testimonials

Want to Work With Us?

Employee of the Week

Tip of the Week

The Future of ____

____ Diaries (Useful blog posts)

Awful ____

Take an Office Tour

Tales of ____

LOL ____ Moments (funny business-related stories)

In the Know... (informative tips, videos, articles)

We LOVE Our ____ (nurses, doctors, consultants, sales people, etc.)

Day Brighteners

Artwork Around Our Digs

Daily Inspiration

The Future of ____

Awesome Inventions

You get the point. While it's likely that you will end up with a mix of broad and narrow boards, the more specific the names, the better. For example instead of naming a board "Travel" that features photos from your trips to India, Japan, and Australia, why not create three separate boards named and focused on that particular country?

Make It Snappy

As mentioned above, board names have a 180-character limit, so you get about seven words or less to get your point across. Keep in mind that when visitors view your profile page, they get a glimpse of all your boards at once. In this, shorter names are better because longer board names may get truncated in the profile view.

Keep It Simple

Clever may be the stuff that Pulitzer Prize-winning novel titles are made of, but abstract, overly crafty, or glib board names will only confuse your audience. By calling your boards what they are in plain English, you stand a better chance of being found by the people who are actually looking for what you offer. This doesn't mean that you can't exercise your creativity. Just keep keywords in mind so that your audience can find you.

Consider Keywords

Keywords are the actual terms, words, and phrases that people type into a search engine to find something. Because Google indexes both your profile and boards, crafting keyword-rich titles can offer a boost to your rankings. Also keep in mind that many people search Pinterest for a specific term(s), so using keywords in your board names that you know your audience searches for will increase your opportunity to be found and followed. To find the best keywords for your boards (as well as pins and descriptions) try the following:

- *Think targeted words and phrases.* Consider how you use search engines in your everyday life. Maybe you type in "puppy potty training tips," "how to program a DVR," or "gluten-free chocolate cake recipes." What all these searches have in common is they contain a straightforward and uncomplicated description of the thing you are looking to find. In short, they are targeted. When coming up with keywords for board names, apply the same idea by:
  - Making a list of your products and services and the various categories they fall under. If a customer was going to look for your business, what keywords might they type into a search engine?

- Thinking about how a customer would describe what you do
- Determining which of your keywords return the best results when typed into a search engine, and which ones are duds

■ *Use the keyword tool in Google AdWords (http://adwords.google.com).* Google AdWords is a fee-based service, but the Keyword Tool is a free, powerful little component that you can use to come up with ideas for new keywords and review the performance figures for each keyword. The Keyword Tool will show you how competitive a keyword is, meaning how often people search for it, both globally and locally.

■ *Check out Google Trends.* Google Trends (http://www.google.com/trends/#) works like any search. Simply enter your keyword into the search box and click "Explore." A graph will appear that shows you that keyword's popularity presently and over time. You will also be able to see related keyword searches ranked by popularity.

Break It Down

Boards that are broad in scope may seem like a great idea as a catchall for a wide variety of pins, but they can diffuse your brand. Decide which of your potential boards are natural candidates for more niched boards. For example, if you run a chic women's boutique, instead of calling a board the more broadly named "Dresses," you might consider creating a series of niched boards such as "Cocktail Party Dresses," "Summer Day Dresses," "Romantic Night Out Dresses," etc. By chunking down your bigger, top-level topics into smaller, more focused boards, you can take advantage of your user's targeted interests.

CATEGORIZE YOUR BOARDS FOR CLARITY

Along with naming your board, you will be asked to select a category for it. For all you eager beavers reading this: No, you cannot skip this step. Pinterest requires that you assign every board you create—regardless of the name you give it—a designated category. Pinterest offers 33 different categories of boards:

- Architecture
- Art
- Cars and Motorcycles
- Design
- DIY and Crafts
- Education
- Film, Music, and Books
- Fitness
- Food and Drink
- Gardening
- Geek
- Hair and Beauty

- History
- Holidays
- Home Décor
- Humor
- Kids
- My Life
- Women's Apparel
- Men's Apparel
- Outdoors
- People
- Pets
- Photography
- Prints and Posters
- Products
- Science and Nature
- Sports
- Technology
- Travel and Places
- Weddings and Events
- Video
- Other

GO SOLO OR INVITE OTHERS TO PLAY

Now that you have done the heavy lifting of deciding what type of board to create, what to call it, and which category it fits into, you also get to determine whether it's going to be a solo or collaborative effort.

CATEGORIES COUNT

A quick tip about categorizing boards: Please be as accurate as you can. The more congruent your boards are with their assigned categories, and the more the pins on those boards match the category, the more credibility you will have and the easier it will be for other pinners to find the content they are looking for. For example, let's say you have a board named "Fun Travel Gadgets" that's a mix of pins including your Dachshund doing cute things with a travel pillow, luggage you love, and great head-phones for listening to the inflight entertainment. The dog, while funny, is off-brand from what people will expect to see on that board. Better to create a second board titled "Crazy Things My Dog Does" and pin the images there.

But what about those situations in which no board category offered seems to fit? One glaring omission from Pinterest as of the writing of this book is that while they allow a business or brand to join as such, they have no "Business" category. If you can't find a suitable category for a business topic, some best bets include: "Technology," "Education," or the always favorite "Other."

Just below the board category box is the "Who Can Pin" option. If you want to be the only pinner for this board, skip the "Invite" box and go straight to clicking the red "Create Board" button. But if you want to invite other, specific pinners to guest pin on the board, you can add the name or email address of the other pinner.

Pinterest will then offer you a list of potential matches. Select the proper persona, and hit the "Invite" button on the far right. You can add as many contributors as you like to a board by following the process outlined above, before clicking on the red "Create Board" button.

One point of Pin-etiquette: The polite thing to do is to ask another person if they would like to be added as a pinner to your board (and wait for an answer) before adding them. For a more extensive and expansive look at how to use Pinterest boards for collaboration, see Chapter 11.

Once you're done deciding whether your board will be a solo or collaborative effort, just select the red "Create Board" button at the bottom of the text box—and you are ready to take the next step in branding your boards.

MAKE YOUR BOARD PRIVATE

What about pins that you want to be able to view at any time, but don't want the general public to see? Pinterest offers a "Secret Boards" option that limits viewing to only the content curator and any guest pinners whom they have invited.

To take advantage of this feature click the "Add+" button from the menu bar, and choose "Create a Board." Locate the "Secret Button" and switch it to the "On" position.

You can also create a private board right from your homepage. Scroll down to the bottom, below all your current boards, and just under the "Create a Board" box, you will see the "Create a Secret Board" box. Click and you will be taken though the process to create a secret board.

One note. When you add a pin to a secret board, it won't show up anywhere else on Pinterest—the only place you can see it is on your "Secret Board." The official Pinterest blog explains that the reason for this is that other people may have already repinned images from those boards. Here are some of the situations in which you might find a private board useful:

- Pins of holiday presents you are considering buying employees, clients, or vendors
- In-house, company, or department-only brainstorming and discussion on a designated topic
- To plan special events that aren't yet ready for public consumption
- Work on private projects (marketing, research, product development, sales, etc.) that you don't want competitors or customers to see

Bear in mind that you are only permitted to have three private boards, so use the option sparingly.

DESCRIBE YOUR BOARD

Once your board has been officially created, you need to give it a description. Go to the drop-down menu under your name in the toolbar and choose "Boards."

Find your newly created board and click on the "Edit Board" function at the bottom. The screen that pops up contains a text box titled "Description," where you can write a brief overview about the board.

Remember to hit "Save Settings" at the end. Just as you would with your title, keep in mind that using keywords in your description can help your SEO efforts, as well as entice visitors to give your board a look-see.

BASIC CARE AND FEEDING OF YOUR BOARDS

Pinterest boards are not static entities, so once they are set up, you can always go back and edit or delete them at any time. Here are a few board housekeeping items.

Rearranging Your Boards

If you want to reorganize the order in which your boards appear, simply place your cursor over your name in the main toolbar in the top right corner of your screen and select "Boards" from the drop-down menu. You will now be able to see all your boards. Located just above your boards and smack dab in the middle of the page is the "Edit Profile" button. Immediately next to that button is a small box button. Selecting this button will enable you to rearrange your boards by dragging them into whatever order you wish. When done, click the red checkmark button that appears between the "Edit Profile" button and the rearrange box to save your changes (see Figure 4–7).

Choosing a Board Cover Image

As soon as you start populating a particular board with pins, Pinterest will automatically take the first image you post and make it that board's default cover. You can change the cover image anytime you like by choosing another pin on that same board. To edit your board photo, click on your name from the homepage and choose "Boards" from the

Get Started	14 Boards	70 Pins	90 Likes	Activity	Edit Profile ⬚		112 Followers	49 Following

FIGURE 4–7. Rearrange Your Boards

drop-down menu. Next, place your cursor over the board image you want to edit and the "Edit Board Cover" text will automatically appear. Click, and another image will pop up with an arrow to the right and left. Scroll through the images on your board until you find the one you want, then adjust which part of the image you want to show in the thumbnail (most board cover images get cropped by Pinterest) and hit the red "Set Cover" button.

Editing Your Boards

Place your cursor over your name in the main toolbar in the top right corner of your screen and select "Boards" from the drop-down menu. You will now be able to see all your boards. Beneath each individual board is an "Edit" button. Select the "Edit" button for the board you wish to change. From here, you will be able to rename the board, change the description, and change the category it is in. You can also make the board collaborative by adding guest pinners. To save changes, select the red "Save Settings" button at the bottom of the screen.

Deleting Your Boards

If you decide one or more of your boards are best suited for the scrap heap, take heart. It's easy to delete any of your boards at any time.

Place your cursor over your name in the main toolbar in the top right corner of your screen and select "Boards" from the drop-down menu. You will now be able to see all your boards. Beneath each individual board is an "Edit" button. Select the "Edit" button for the board you wish to delete. Next to the title of the board is a white "Delete Board" button.

Select it, and a secondary window pops up, asking you if you're sure you want to permanently delete your board. If you're sure, click the red "Delete Board" button. Once you delete a board, it can't be undone, so if you want to think about it a bit more, click "Cancel" to go back to the board's edit page.

Having so carefully created your on-brand boards in this chapter, it's time to roll up your sleeves and get on to the heart of the Pinterest experience—curating content.

One word of advice here. If you're tempted to skip the next chapter (and all the work of finding great content to pin) and just head straight for finding followers— don't. It's critical to populate the boards you have just created with content, i.e., pins, first. There's no point in driving people to your Pinterst page if there's nothing, or very little, for them to see. So take your time, do this right, and pin killer content. In the long run this will make you more effective at gaining followers who are really engaged with your brand.

Chapter 5

Become a Content Creator and Curator:
Pinning and Repinning

The right boards, beautifully named, won't do you much good if they aren't housing winning pins. And let's face it: The pics (and videos) you post are what will make or break your Pinterest reputation and determine how far you can go. But what pushes a pin past mediocre to being a star player? In short, it's your ability to curate content that is meaningful, attractive, social media friendly, and on message with your brand.

If you are not familiar with the term "content curation," it's a three-part act composed of:

- Searching for and sifting through web content on a particular subject area
- Sorting through, interpreting, and synthesizing that information
- Presenting and, finally, distributing the data in a useful and meaningful way to a given audience

The shorthand way to think about it is to envision the way a museum or art gallery puts together a show on a given artist or subject matter.

If that sounds like a lot to fit on the head of one small pin, it's easier than you think. To curate winning pins, you need to know what to pin; where to find, or how to create, great images; and the mechanics of pinning from various places.

WHAT SHOULD YOU PIN?

Not all pins are created equal. Just posting any old photo or video won't get visitors to follow your boards or find out more about you. In general, you want all your pins to meet the following criteria.

Is It Appropriate?

This may sound obvious, but, as Pinterest states, porn, nudity, graphic violence, attacks on groups or individuals, hateful speech or symbols, and spam are all considered objectionable content. It's very simple: Just don't post them. On a more personal level, be sure to think before you pin anything that might violate another's privacy or your own. A good rule of thumb: If you wouldn't want the image or information to appear on the front page of *The New York Times*, then it doesn't belong on Pinterest.

Is it Interesting, Cute, Unique, Beautiful, and/or Funny?

The only thing a visitor to your Pinterest account may use to determine whether they want to stay is their first glance at the pictures you post. Anyone who has ever read a Match.com profile knows that certain attributes are highly desirable in a potential date. The same goes for Pinterest pins. Pins that are interesting, funny, cute, beautiful, or unique stand a better chance of getting repinned and asked out on a second date. If visitors aren't intrigued enough by the image to go further, they may never get to your bio, click through to your website, or even read the description of the pin.

Is It on Brand, Message, and Target?

A high-end cosmetic dentist's Pinterest boards probably won't feature photos of cute little bunnies lying in the sun—but a veterinarian's site just might. Whatever images you end up pinning, they won't move your marketing forward if they aren't congruent with your brand and on message and on target for your audience. Remember way back in Chapter 3 where you thought through your strategy for Pinterest? Here is where it comes in handy. Don't waste your audience's time or patience with images that don't directly and specifically:

- *Make them happier, healthier, or richer*. GoGirl Finance (http://pinterest.com/gogirlfinance/) has a board called "Personal Finance," which offers a host of "how-to" pins on how to handle your money, including one on "5 Ways to Help (or Hurt) Your Credit Score."
- *Move and/or inspire them*. Check out the "Happiness" board from Passion and Positivity (http://pinterest.com/positiveiquotes/), which focuses on aspirational messages and images.

- *Show them how to do something better, faster, cheaper, etc.* Fitness magazine (http://pinterest.com/fitnessmagsa/) has a whole board titled "Work Those Abs," with pins showing ways to get tight and toned.
- *Educate, enlighten, or entertain them.* Dr. Mehmet Oz (http://pinterest.com/doctoroz/), of *Oprah* fame, has a strong presence on Pinterest, with more than 100,000 followers. His "Oz Lists" board offers educational information on healthy foods such as the "100 Foods Dr. Oz Wants in Your Grocery Cart" pin.

Likewise, spending your efforts posting things that help craft an accurate and powerful picture of who you are as a business and brand makes viewers want to further engage with you.

Do Your Pins Tell a Story, with Feeling?

A picture is worth a thousand words. Photos that evoke a strong emotion, tell a story, or communicate a clear message make great pins. One way to evaluate whether your image has the right stuff is to think of a single word that expresses the idea, meaning, story, or message you want to convey. Then take that word and find images that match.

The Right Size

While Pinterest doesn't limit the vertical size of the image you can post, it only allows for a horizontal width of 600 pixels. Anything wider will be resized. However, it's best to avoid a long vertical that requires visitors to scroll down to view the entire image. Instead, keep your vertical size to under 5,000 pixels. On the other side of the coin, images that are too small (under 250 pixels wide or deep) end up looking teeny-tiny and don't catch the eye.

The Right Mix

While there are no hard-and-fast rules about pin content composition, the general idea is to mix it up enough so that your boards are robust, not boring. While Pinterest is more art than science, a good rule of thumb for the percentage of pins that should make up your boards is:

- *40 percent motivational.* These are pins that uplift and inspire. They may be motivational quotes, moving images, or beautiful photographs, but they create a desire in the viewer for something more, better, higher.
- *40 percent instructional.* Educational rather than promotional in nature, these are pins that show the viewer how to do something related to your brand or topic. For example, makeup application techniques are one of the most popular types of pins on the site.

- *10 percent product or service profiles.* Pins that feature your products and/or services and promote your business do have a place on Pinterest—but they should not be the majority of what your pins are about. Pins that feature offers, contests, specials, and demonstrations of what you do belong to this group.
- *10 percent about the brand.* These are pins that tell your story, your company story, and the story of your brand. Pins that profile your customers, feature people engaging with your products or services, and highlight testimonials for your company, etc., fit into this category.

Keep in mind that these percentages can change based on the type of business you have and the demands of your audience.

SEEK AND YE SHALL FIND: WHERE TO GET GREAT PINS

Now that you have an idea of the kind of content you want to pin, where do you find these fabulous images? Everywhere, fortunately. According to webanalyticsworld.net, the internet plays host to just under half a trillion images.

Of course, not all of those are up for grabs (see Chapter 6 for copyright concerns), but there are plenty to go around. You just need to know where to look. The trick is to hit that magical mix of pinning your own stuff, pinning other people's (and companies') available images, and repinning what others have already pinned.

Shop Your Current Images

Remember that scene at the end of *The Wizard of Oz* where Dorothy says (and I'm paraphrasing here, for all you die-hards) that if she ever again goes looking for her heart's desire, she won't go any further than her own backyard? As you think of places where you can find pins, keep that piece of musical movie wisdom in mind and search for images close to home, including:

- Logos, diagrams, drawings, pictures, models, videos, and other visual content on your website or blog that you could pin
- Logos, diagrams, drawings, pictures, models, videos, and other visual content used in your business (but not up on your website) that could be turned into a web image and pinned
- Photos and videos you have taken and own the copyright to that you would be willing to post.
- Photos and videos friends and family members have taken that they own the copyright to and will give you permission to use (with credit, of course)

- Photos and videos that employees have taken that you or they own the copyright to and that they will give you permission to use (with credit)
- Videos you've already posted on YouTube that would be right for your Pinterest site. By the way, video is so important that it warrants its own chapter in this book (Chapter 7, "Beyond Photos to Video, Podcasts, and Screencasting").
- Photos or videos of things you are selling. Whether the item is something hand-made and created by you (art, craft, hobby) or a mass-manufactured product, take a photo of the item and pin and promote it.
- Individual slides from decks you have already created via PowerPoint presentations can be saved as jpegs to your desktop and then uploaded as a pin—one image at a time.

Generate New Infographics and Text Images

Text-based images and infographics are everywhere on Pinterest and provide your business with a more engaging way to present numbers, facts, statistics, and findings. There are a plethora of free or low-cost tools available on the web to help you generate your own images including:

- *Shareasimage.com.* This site lets you highlight text anywhere on the web and easily convert it to an image you can pin. The tool offers both a free and low-cost professional version. The paid version allows you to choose fonts, colors, and text size.
- *Imagechef.com* offers a no-charge bundle of image creation tools all in one stop including customized text sticky notes, word mosaics, and a poetry blender that lets you combine text, symbols, and photos.
- *infogr.am/* provides a simple way to turn your data into an infographic. The choice of templates is limited, but for presenting numbers and statistics in a picture form quickly, and for free, this app works well.
- *Piktochart.com* offers more interesting themes for infographics than some of their competitors, but choices for the free version are limited. The paid version for more serious infographic creators offers 80 professional themes and additional customization for a nominal monthly fee.
- *Pinstamatic.com* is a great one-stop shop for image creation. This site allows you to generate quotes, edit photos, easily take screenshots of websites, pin your favorite songs and album covers, add pins of Twitter profiles, add captions to your favorite photos, and create cool photo collages.
- *Someecards.com.* Lately these have been showing up all over Pinterest. The site lets you grab existing cards to pin, but also gives you the opportunity to create your own. Their old-fashioned illustrated look makes them a standout.

Find Images to Repin by Searching Topics

Browsing the "Categories" section located on the homepage of Pinterest is one way to discover new content you can potentially repin. However, these are fairly broad, so narrow your browsing to a more specific topic by using the search function in the menu bar. Enter the keyword you want to find in the "Search" box, located at the top left corner of your screen, and click the magnifying glass next to the "Search" box (or press "Enter"). You will then see a page containing the pins most relevant to your search topic. If you want to find the most relevant boards to your search topic, click the "Boards" link, located at the top of your results. You will be taken to a new page displaying the boards most pertinent to your topic—sorted by user. For example, if you enter the term "Social Media" into the "Search" box and click on "Boards," those boards that have the term "Social Media" in their title will come up.

Find Images to Repin by Searching Users

You can also use the search function to find specific pinners. For example, let's say you are interested in seeing what celebrity chef Paula Deen or retailer Nordstrom has been pinning. Enter the name of the person or company you're looking for into the "Search" box (e.g., Ellen DeGeneres, Banana Republic, *The New York Times*) and you will be shown pins that match your query. Companies and institutions are treated like people on Pinterest, so to filter by people only, click the "Pinners" link at the top left of the search results. The new page will then only display pinners who match your search. Likewise, you can search for pins specifically from the stream of pinners you have chosen to follow.

Find Images to Repin by Searching Hashtags

Pinterest allows users to add hashtags (#word) to their individual pins so they can be more easily found via keyword search. To find images that meet the keyword criteria you're looking for, go to the "Search" box and enter the hashtag symbol followed by the specific word or phrase you want. For example: Let's say you own a party planning company and are looking to pin images related to the Fourth of July. A search for #fourthofjuly (no spaces between words) brings up a whole host of images you can choose from for repinning related to that keyword phrase. In addition, anytime you are on a pin that shows a hashtag in the pin description, just click on it and you will be taken to the search results for other pins containing that same hashtag.

Find Images to Repin by Searching Most Popular

Click "Popular" from the top menu of the homepage, and the pins that have the most comments, likes, and repins will appear. From here you can pick and choose any that

JUST FOR FUN

The rise of the visual web has led to a whole host of ways to create silly, fun, and whimsical images, such as www.keepcalm-o-matic.co.uk. Here you can take the popular WWII poster "Keep Calm and Carry On" and make your own saying—and then instantly pin it (see the figure below).

Keep Calm and Pin On

might be right for your boards. One word of caution—well, two. First, just because a pin is popular doesn't mean that it is a good fit with your brand or business. Second, uber-popular pins reach a point where they become online noise and lead to viewer burnout. So if a pin has hit its popularity peak, meaning when you log in and look at most popular, it's spamming the front page, you may want to think twice before using it.

Find Images to Repin While Browsing

According to a 2012 study by RJMetrics, more than 80 percent of pins are repins. Compare this with a similar study done on Twitter, where only about 1.4 percent of tweets were retweets, and the importance of repinning becomes obvious. If you're surfing Pinterest and you run across something cool you want to capture, it's easy to repin on the run.

Hover your cursor over the image you want to capture and click "Repin." A new window will pop up, allowing you to choose which board you would like to pin the image to. Click the drop-down menu and select the appropriate board. You can always move the image to a different board at a later date. The image will more than likely come with a description from the previous pinner, which you can feel free to use as is or replace with your own description of the pin. To finalize, click the red "Pin It" button.

Find Images to Repin by Searching Gifts

Located at the top menu of the home bar, the "Gifts" option offers a drop-down menu of items specifically available for purchase by price category ranging from $1 all the way up to $500 plus. Clicking on the "Gifts" link alone, without selecting a price category from the drop-down menu, will take you straight to a page displaying gift pins of various prices.

Find Images to Pin from the Web

Keeping copyright issues in mind, the web offers up a whole host of images you can possibly pin. By far the easiest method to achieve this is to install the Pinterest "Pin It" button on your browser, which allows you to easily grab an image from a website and pin it to one of your boards. Alternatively you can pin an image found on a website from within Pinterest—as long as you have the permalink URL for the image you want to pin. Instructions for both methods follow in the "The Mechanics of Pinning" section of this chapter.

DON'T BE A HOARDER

If you're already on Pinterest, chances are you've run across several pinners whose pins and boards look remarkably alike. While there is no set cap on the number of repins you can make from another pinner's boards, it's just plain old rude (and lazy) to be a hoarder and rely on repinning a bunch of someone else's content.

Find Images to Pin on Royalty-Free Photo Sites

As long as the images you are posting are for noncommercial use, there are scads of websites out there offering royalty-free, reasonably priced (or free) photos that can be pinned. If you're not familiar with the term, "royalty-free" means images that don't require you to pay each time you use them. Instead you pay a one-time fee upfront (and sometimes nothing), and agree to keep your usage to noncommercial or limited impressions.

One advantage of these sites is that they are stocked with images from many amateur—yet creative and talented—photographers. This means you can end up with an image to pin that is more interesting and unusual, which is a good thing in the Pinterest world. Again—and I don't mean to be a nag here—please practice credit where credit is due and give full linkage and acknowledgment to the image's creator when pinning. For some affordable image sites that inspire, check out:

- www.123rf.com
- www.Bigstock.com
- www.Crestock.com
- www.Dreamstime.com
- www.Flickr.com/Creative Commons
- www.Fotolia.com
- www.Morguefile.com
- www.Photodune.net
- www.Stockvault.net
- www.loc.gov/pictures

SHOOT YOUR OWN IMAGES WITH A SMARTPHONE

If you have an image in mind for a particular pin, but it doesn't exist, why not create it? You don't need to be Ansel Adams, Henri Cartier-Bresson, or Annie Leibovitz to shoot a

USE SKITCH TO GARNER SCREENSHOT IMAGES

Skitch (www.skitch.com) is a utility that allows you to take a screenshot of any web page and then share it on Pinterest. Once downloaded and opened, simply click on the "Snap" button in the upper right-hand corner and drag a box around the area of the screen you wish to pin, then release. When you are done selecting the image, it will appear in a box. You can then use the "Drag Me" tag at the bottom of the image and migrate the image to your desktop, where you can go through the process for uploading a pin.

Pinterest-worthy pic. Today's smartphones make it a cinch for amateur photographers to snap and edit shots right in the palm of their hands.

Lynette Sheppard, author, professional photographer, and iPhone photo enthusiast, is the creative voice behind www.iphonediva.com and Lynette Sheppard on Pinterest (http://pinterest.com/lynettesheppard/), where she pins and writes about her own and others' photo art experiments using the iPhone. Sheppard says that 8-megapixel smartphone cameras and the huge variety of apps available for them allow almost anyone to craft not only incredibly sharp and clear photos for Pinterest but to create dramatically visual images as well.

Besides, as the saying goes, "The best camera for the job is the one you have with you," and since most of us are tethered to our phone/camera combos 24/7, what better way to capture images when we are out and about? While Sheppard's passion is iPhone-oriented, her tips that follow on how to make your photos sing on the site work equally well with almost any smartphone.

Think Postcard

Imagine an old-fashioned bulletin board with cool postcards pinned to it. It's the quality and intrigue of those images that make you want to walk up to them and take a look. Think of the photo you are taking as a postcard that will end up on that board, and shoot accordingly.

Keep It Simple

Images on Pinterest show up in a relatively small size, so make sure it's crystal clear what the picture is about. "A big scenic with a lot of people in it isn't going to read well on Pinterest," says Sheppard. "Instead, go for a strong graphic or tightly focused shot."

Fill the Frame with the Focal Point

One of Sheppard's fellow photographers, Rikki Cooke (who teaches photography workshops on the Island of Molokai in Hawaii), tells his students to "Fill the frame with the focal point." In other words, if you're taking a picture of a dog, fill the frame with the dog's face. If you're taking a picture of a flower, don't make the daisy the size of a dot floating in a big background of environment. "Too much competing visual information just doesn't read well in Pinterest photos," says Sheppard.

Crop Liberally

One way to comment on what's really important in an image is to crop it so that the critical visual element becomes the focus of the photograph. Pinterest automatically crops the photos you pin so they fit the site's specs, but bear in mind that the crop adjustments in Pinterest are minimal. So for the best results, crop the image yourself prior to pinning.

Shoot in HDR

Thanks to the advent of high dynamic range (HDR) applications, quality photographs can be shot in almost any light, including high contrast, bright sunshine, and cloud cover. Pro HDR is an easy-to-use app that allows you to take two concurrent photos of the same subject—one focusing on the bright part of the image, one on the dark. The app analyzes the light available, takes the two photos, and combines them for the best image possible. The only thing you need to do is hold the camera steady while the images are being shot. Sheppard uses Pro HDR for most of the photos she pins on her Pinterest site at www.pinterest.com/lynettesheppard.

Go for the "Wow" Factor

Even if you consider yourself a person who doesn't know much about photography, you know a good photo when you see one. Sheppard calls this the "wow" factor. So rather than choosing a photo just because it's from this great place you went, instead find an image you shot of the place that has you going "wow" yourself and post that one. Sheppard suggests looking at other pins that you think have the "wow" factor and mimicking their style and composition. "That's how most artists do things to start," says Sheppard. "We imitate."

Use an All-Around Photo-Optimizing App

Perfect for the amateur photographer, an app such as Perfectly Clear can be used with both the iPhone and Android. The app cleans up the photo (sharpening, brightening) while it's still in your phone before posting.

Consider Black and White

While color photographs make up the majority of what people post on Pinterest, Sheppard says there is a place for dramatic black and white images as well. The app

WATERMARK YOUR WORK

If you're going to take your own photographs, it's in your best interest to protect your images by watermarking them. A watermark is a faint logo or word(s) overlaid on a photo—usually placed at the bottom or off in a lower corner, where it won't obscure the image. Watermarks can be:

- A simple copyright symbol
- A logo-based image
- Text such as your name or business name

Whichever type you choose, watermarks prevent others from copying or using your photo without your permission, and, in the event of repinning, keep the credit for the photo clearly visible.

There are numerous free or inexpensive programs around that allow you to add watermarks to your work, but when it comes to user-friendliness, not all programs are created equal.

For the iPhone, the Impression app is ridiculously simple to use and produces a simple, nonintrusive watermark. For use on your desktop, one of the easiest to use is WaterMark.ws. It's free, offers a video tutorial, and, unlike many other watermarking programs, doesn't require you to download any software. Rather, you upload your photos to the site and complete the processing online.

You can use this site to watermark any images in jpg, jpeg, png, gif, bmp, tif, or tiff; images are limited to 500 KB. To watermark images over 500 KB, you would need to upgrade to WaterMark Pro, a paid service.

Simply B&W elegantly turns color photos into black and white with options for brightness, contrast, framing, and more. "It's like having a little Ansel Adams in your phone," says Sheppard.

Have Fun with Filters

If you're looking for a one-stop-shop app with an abundance of filters, Sheppard recommends FX Photo Studio, which offers 194 photo effects that allow you to turn ordinary photos into Pinterest masterpieces.

THE MECHANICS OF PINNING

There are four main methods you can use to populate your various boards. All are relatively easy and fast, so pick an option and pin away.

Option 1: The "Pin It" Button

Adding a "Pin It" button to your web browser streamlines posting and allows you to pin on the go while surfing the web. The first step is to install the button onto your web browser toolbar. Instructions for how to do this vary by browser, but the Pinterest website offers easy-to-follow step-by-step installation instructions for each main browser.

To access the instructions, hover your cursor over the "About" drop-down menu in the main toolbar, located at the top right corner of the screen. Select the "Pin It" button from the menu. You will then be taken to a page with step-by-step instructions for installing the button, as well as a video tutorial. The instructions are already customized for the web browser in which you are currently operating. Follow the directions to install the button.

Once you have the "Pin It" button installed, pinning while browsing becomes a snap since the "Pin It" button is actually a bookmark that can be accessed from your bookmarks toolbar. First, make sure you're logged into Pinterest. Then, go to the page you want to pin and click the "Pin It" button, visible on your bookmark toolbar. A page will pop up showing the pinnable images available and their sizes in pixels. Hover your cursor over the image you want to pin, and a "Pin It" button will appear in the center of that image. Click the button, and a "Create Pin" window will pop up, displaying the image. Next, choose the board you want to pin the image to and give the pin a new description. Select the red "Pin It" button to finalize. By the way, when you pin from a website, Pinterest automatically grabs the source link so the original creator is given proper credit.

Option 2: Add a Pin

If you want to pin an image from a website and either don't have the "Pin It" button installed on your browser or it's not returning the images you want, you can pin directly from a website URL using the "Add a Pin" button on Pinterest.

From the Pinterest homepage, locate the "Add+" button on the upper right-hand side of your main menu bar. Click, and a dialog box titled "Add" will pop up. Once the mini-panel is open, click the "Add a Pin" button, which is illustrated by the graphic of a thumbtack.

You will then be directed to copy and paste the URL of the website page that you'd like to pin into the text box.

Once you've entered the URL, click the "Find Images" button to the right. A panel will appear in the lower left-hand corner, below the URL, which displays a mini-slideshow of the pinnable images from the site you have just accessed.

Use the "Prev" and "Next" buttons below the image to scroll through until you find the one you want to pin. Next, use the drop-down bar to select the board you want to pin the image to and enter a new description of the pin.

Pinterest gives you the option to have the new pin promoted to Twitter and/or Facebook (or not). Lastly, click the red "Pin It" button, and voila! You've just added that image to your designated board.

Option 3: Upload a Pin

You can also upload a jpeg image that lives on your computer desktop. From the homepage of Pinterest, locate the "Add+" button on the upper right-hand side of your main menu bar. Click, and a dialog box titled "Add" will pop up. Once the mini panel is open, select "Upload a Pin," illustrated by an upward-facing arrow graphic (see Figure 5–1).

Click the "Browse" button to locate the image on your hard drive; select the image, and a dialog with the image in the lower right-hand corner will appear. Next, use the drop-down bar to select the board you want to pin the image to and enter a new description of the pin.

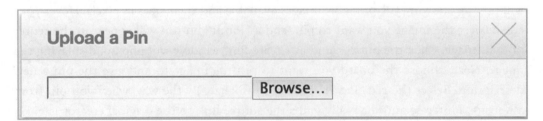

FIGURE 5–1. Upload a Pin

You can then choose to have the new pin promoted to Twitter and/or Facebook (or not). Lastly, click the red "Pin It" button. This method of pinning does not automatically provide a link to the pin, so after you upload the image, go back in and edit the pin to add a URL link back to an appropriate source.

Option 4: Repin from within Pinterest

As you are browsing Pinterest, you will no doubt come across images that you want to pin. No problem. Like retweeting on Twitter, you can repin another user's image onto one of your boards. Place your cursor over the image you want to repin, and three buttons will pop up, one of which is "Repin." Click the "Repin" button, and the dialog box that appears offers a drop-down menu of your boards. Choose which board you want to add the pin to, or create a new board, and type in a new description of the repin in the text box provided.

Finding great images puts you on the right path for Pinterest success, but once you know what you want to pin, your next challenge is to optimize those pins for performance.

Pin Etiquette
and Optimization

Regardless of where you find your pins, your job as a citizen of Pinterest nation is to respect the rules of the community and optimize your pins for peak performance. As Mashable community assistant Jeremy Cabalona pointed out on a recent Infographic, "A properly optimized pin can make all the difference between 50 repins or no repins." If you follow these best practices for pinning and repinning, you will protect your Pinterest reputation and get the most out of social media scrapbooking.

PIN PURPOSEFULLY

Have you ever gone into an electronics (or shoe) store and been so enthralled by the selection of available goods that you were tempted to just throw caution to the wind and buy more than you should? Of course you have. Avoid approaching Pinterest like a kid in a candy store and stuffing your boards with images that look nice, but don't really fit your brand or business. The key is to be selective in what you pin and only pin the most compelling and relevant content. Taking into consideration the Pinterest strategy you set early on (Chapter 3) will help you determine what images will make the cut.

ADD DESCRIPTIONS

One surefire way to optimize your pins for search is by giving each one a spot-on description that includes your relevant keywords. There is a 500-character limit for descriptions, so be deliberate in what you write—and follow these guidelines for making your descriptions count.

Provide a Context

Images without descriptions leave it to the user's imagination as to why you pinned that particular item or what point you were trying to make. Granted, some images are so breathtaking that they need no explanation. However, in most cases, a clear, concise, and specific description of a pin can help pique a user's interest. Items to consider when writing a description include:

- What you specifically liked about the image
- Why you pinned the image
- What idea the image represents
- What tips you have that go along with the image
- What opinions you have about the image
- Additional information related to the image

Spell out the Specifics

Images that have vague descriptions are less useful for the viewer than those that spell out the specifics. For example, let's say you have a pin showing a selection of great office gifts to give clients. A description that reads, "These are really great to give as client gifts," is less impactful than one that says, "These five gifts, all under $30, can be used by a man or a woman and are something every small-business person needs. For this reason, they make great holiday client gifts. Here's a link to where you can buy them." Now that's a useful description.

Link to Your Website

You can add live links to the captions below your pins simply by adding a URL to a pin's description and clicking the red "Save Pin" button. Adding a link to the description encourages people to click through and drives traffic to your website and/or blog.

Include a Call to Action

According to a study by Reachli.com (formerly known as Pinerly), descriptions that contain a call to action see an 80 percent increase in engagement.

For example, let's say you've pinned an image for tax season that shows a small-business owner pulling out his hair in despair. The description explains that there are five ways a small business can avoid stress at tax time and provides a link to an article on the topic. That's a good start, but you take it one step further by encouraging viewers with a specific call to action with a simple sentence or two. Here are some suggested call-to-action phrases you can incorporate into your pin descriptions as appropriate:

- Download the free ebook.
- Read more ways to . . .
- To learn more . . .
- Sign up online.
- Ask the experts.
- For more details . . .
- Please submit ideas and questions to . . .
- Win a free . . .
- Call for a complimentary consultation.
- Get a free quote.
- Tell us what you think.
- I'd love to hear your comments and feedback.
- Watch a video of . . .

Add Testimonials

A good strategy for both product and service businesses is to include testimonials in your pin descriptions. For example, if you have a pin showcasing a garden your landscaping company overhauled, you might want to place a short quote from the happy homeowner in the description.

One word of caution on testimonials: In a recent case concerning Nutrisystem and Pinterest, The Better Business Bureau's National Advertising Division (NAD) ruled that the company needed to make the same disclosures on Pinterest that they are required to make in other types of advertising. Specifically, the NAD shook their finger at Nutrisystem for a campaign they featured on a Pinterest page showing people who had lost a great deal of weight. The diet company's "Member Spotlight" board now features testimonials—accompanied by the familiar "results not typical" disclosure.

Use Keywords

One important aspect of SEO (search engine optimization) is the inclusion of keywords and phrases your target audience is searching for. By using these sparingly and strategically in your pin descriptions, you can increase your Google rankings but also be more discoverable by users searching Pinterest for a particular topic. For more details on how to find Keywords check out Chapter 4 on building boards.

Be Mindful of Description Etiquette

Bear in mind that the description etiquette changes depending on whether the pin is yours, a repin, or sourced from somewhere on the web.

Repins

Whenever you repin an image, Pinterest automatically brings the description over as well. If that description fits, fine—you can leave it as it is or even just add a few words of your own to personalize it. However, in some cases, you may find it more advantageous to write a new description.

For example, I found a great photo featuring puzzle-piece cookies on a food board by another pinner. I loved the photo, but I wanted to use it on my Personal Productivity and Time Management Board to make a point about how we are trying to fit all the puzzle pieces of our lives together. Hence, I repinned the image (giving credit to the original pinner), but I rewrote the description to fit my purposes.

Pinning from a Website

Take note! When pinning from a specific blog post, permalink URL, or website, avoid copying and pasting the given description verbatim to avoid copyright infringement. For example, some pinners have violated food bloggers' intellectual property by copying and pasting the blogger's recipes into the comment box. Be original and write your own descriptions, while being sure to credit and link back to the original source.

PLACE A PIN DESCRIPTION ON THE SPOT

If you're on a website and find an image you want to pin, you can pick up a few lines of the text automatically. Simply highlight the portion of the text you want to use before clicking "Pin It" and the text will be placed in that pin's description. Remember: It's key to give proper attribution, so be sure to edit the description once you pin it by putting the text in quotation marks and adding a note to the description directing people back to the original source.

PAY ATTENTION TO PIN PLACEMENT

Since the images you pin on your boards can be arranged in any way you choose (vs. a chronological order of which pin came first, second, etc.), you want to organize your pins in a way that tells the best story for that topic and creates the most user engagement.

To that end, consider the work of EyeTrackShop (http://eyetrackshop.com/). General manager Jeff Bander and his team have conducted more than 350,000 studies using webcam eye-tracking technology to observe and measure the way people view their screens.

One EyeTracksShop study conducted for Mashable.com tracked the eye movements of 600 participants as they viewed top Pinterest pages at 10-second intervals and then answered a survey about each page they had viewed. The findings provide some insight that can influence pin placement.

Front and Center

Bander and his team found that most Pinterest viewers' eyes followed a pattern from the top down to the middle of the page. Hence, pins that were placed front and center received the highest percentage of viewers. Translated into placement strategy, this means your most important, compelling, or interesting pins should live around the middle, top, or second row of the board they sit on.

Faces Trump Objects

Although an enormous amount of the images found on Pinterest are of things and not people, respondents in the study tended to look at faces and areas of a board that contained faces more often than those containing other images. "Neurologically, we are wired to be attracted to faces," says Bander. "The faces were the first thing people looked at on Pinterest in our study."

Bander recommends one of two approaches to pinning faces on Pinterest:

- *Emotion based.* Decide on the kind of emotion you want to evoke from your audience and/or have represent your brand, and then set about to find photos of faces that are associated with that emotion.
- *Ambiguous.* "If you really want people to spend more time looking at a face, make the expression ambiguous," says Bander. Think of the Mona Lisa. The brain can't quite figure it out, so it spends more time trying to analyze it.

Bander says the big lesson to learn here is that whether you go with an emotion-based or ambiguous face, it's important to prominently place at least some pictures of people onto your boards, then place the other image-based pins you want people to look at in close proximity.

Brand Pages Matter

The EyeTrackShop study also found that profile pages of actual brands, such as Coca-Cola, were just as popular as category pages, such as food. In fact, participants were slightly more likely to repin images they saw on brand and individual pages than on category pages.

"Companies can take this as a sign that the strength of their brand on Pinterest really does matter," says Bander. "The more specific and unique a company can make their boards to their business, vs. generic pins, the more likely they are to engage their viewers."

Viewing Pages Increases Brand Appreciation

The people in the study reported having a higher opinion of the brand, and being more likely to purchase something, after having viewed the Pinterest pages.

CONSIDER COLOR PSYCHOLOGY WHEN PINNING

Color is a critical element in how you design your website and present your brand. Studies from the Institute for Color Research show that people make a subconscious judgment about a person, environment, or product within 90 seconds of initial viewing, and that between 62 percent and 90 percent of that assessment is based on color alone. Another study from the University of Loyola, Maryland, found that color increases brand recognition by up to 80 percent.

But how do you know what colors will resonate with your Pinterest followers? "Different colors evoke different emotions," says EyeTrackShop's Bander. One of their studies focused on the emotions that different colors inspire. So, if you are looking to keep your pins on target—with the right tint—consider these color psychology guidelines, which originally appeared on a blog post I wrote for Intuit.com's small business blog (http://blog.intuit.com/).

- *Red*. Full of energy, it's a rich color that sits up and says, "Take notice of me." It inspires impulse purchases. Beware: It also can mean "warning" and "danger," so use soberly.
- *Orange*. Evokes a sense of fun and comfort. Bright like the sun, it draws attention for calls to action.
- *Yellow*. Seen by the human eye as the brightest color, yellow is a cheerful attention grabber that is often used to designate a sale or special offer. Warning: Yellow text on a white background can be hard to read.

UPDATE YOUR DESCRIPTIONS ANYTIME

In the event that you decide someday to go back and alter your description, you can easily do so by signing into Pinterest, hovering over you name in the upper right-hand corner of the page, and selecting pins from the drop-down menu. A page will appear with all your pins. Find the pin whose description you want to edit, place your cursor over the image, and click the "Edit" button that appears at the top. A text box showing the board, description, and links associated with the pin will appear. Change the description as desired and then click the red "Save Pin" button.

- *Green.* The easiest color on the eyes, it brings out a feeling of balance and is seen as restful and happy, associated with nature. Often used in logos because it shouts "stability."
- *Blue.* Engenders trust and loyalty. Because the energy of blue communicates security and stability, it's the dominant color of choice for many conservative, corporate websites.
- *Purple.* Bringing to mind an image of royalty and luxury, purple is a power color that can bring drama to an aspect of your online message.
- *White.* The blank slate and the clean start, white is the stabilizing influence, the color that brings balance. "Whatever colors you choose, allow plenty of white space," says Whitney Holden, co-founder of Zodiac digital design studio. "To avoid brightness/contrast issues, use a white background with interesting splashes of color to highlight important information."
- *Black.* A stock color for those seeking sophistication in their message, black can also read as glamorous and powerful. When used in contrast with other colors, it makes a strong statement.

CROSS-PROMOTE YOUR PINS WITH OTHER SOCIAL MEDIA

If you really want your efforts on Pinterest to have an impact on the overall marketing of your business and building of your brand, I have two words for you: cross promotion.

Pinterest works best when it shares the social media stage with Facebook, Twitter, and your blog. Here are some simple ways to do just that.

Get a Pinterest Tab for Your Facebook Page

This allows you to show your boards and pins via a specific tab on Facebook and makes your Pinterest presence more visible across platforms.

Check out Woobox, an app that lets you customize the features of the tab. For example, using Woobox, you can enable a setting that requires users to "like" your Facebook page before they will be permitted to view your Pinterest tab. You can also use Woobox as a means to track analytics and view complete statistics for page views, visits, and likes, and organize them by fans and non-fans who view your tab.

Connect Pinterest to Your Facebook Timeline

When you log into Pinterest, go to the drop-down menu under your photo. Choose the settings tab and locate the Facebook tab with the "On and Off" switch. Set the button to "On" and it will bring up a text box asking for your user name (or email), and password. Log in and you will be taken to your Facebook page, where you will have the option of clicking the "Log In with Facebook" button. Click it and your Facebook and Pinterest accounts will be connected. You can then go back to your settings in Pinterest and will see a "Publish Activity To Facebook Timeline" button. Move that button to the "On" position, and you're good to go.

Use Your Facebook Status Updates

If you have a pin (or board) you are particularly excited about, just copy and paste the pin's URL into your status update box and hit "Enter." You will then be able to see the image, board title, and caption of the pin. Be selective in using this method, since an over-promotion of pins to Facebook can feel like spam to your friends.

Like a Pin on Facebook

To have a pin automatically show up in your status update on Facebook, open it to its full size and click the "Like" button on the right. This will populate the image, description, and board name for your Facebook friends to see.

Like a Board on Facebook

In addition to liking an individual pin, you can also like a board. Open the board you want to post on Facebook and locate the blue "Like" button next to the board's title. Click, and a text box appears in which you can write a comment and post to your Facebook timeline.

Post Your Pins to Twitter

Each full-size version of your pins has a blue Twitter icon located to the right. Clicking on that button tweets that particular pin. You can also tweet pins as you create them by checking the small Twitter box (to the right of the red "Pin It" button).

Embed a Pin in Your Blog

There may be those occasions when you want a particular pin to be embedded in your blog. Open the pin to its full size and click on the "Embed" button to the right. A text box will pop up with the code that you copy and paste directly into your blog or onto a page on your website.

Share a Pin Via Email

Open the individual pin you want to its full size and locate the "Email" button on the right. A text box appears in which you can enter the recipient's name, email, and a message. Hit "Send," and your pin is on its way.

CREDIT ORIGINAL SOURCES

If you pin an image or video that was created by someone else, Pinterest etiquette (and common courtesy) obligates you to give the credit back to the original source via a link. This, as you will discover, isn't always as easy as it seems. There are two scenarios that occur when crediting a source.

Images Pinned Directly from the Web Get Automatically Sourced

If you pin an image from a website, it will automatically generate a link back to the URL from whence it came—and proper sourcing credit will have been achieved.

Images Taken from a Website, but Placed on Your Desktop

There are times when you will find an image on another website, but, for various reasons (sizing, adjustment), will place it on your desktop. When you upload that image from your computer, Pinterest will automatically issue the credit to you, not the source. The easy solution is to edit the pin once it's been placed by adding to its description the URL of the image's original source.

For more specifics on this subject, read on to the copyright information.

RESPECT COPYRIGHT

Full warning before you read this section: In the same way that a diet book warns you to check with a doctor before proceeding and not to take what is written as medical advice, the information that follows is not and should not be construed as legal advice. Since varying circumstances may make something copyright-free or copyright-protected, when in doubt, check with your attorney. Also, if you sense a change in tone for this part of the book, you would be correct. Sorry, folks; there is just no way to make all this legal stuff sound conversational, let alone sexy.

With those warnings out of the way, the following is meant as a general guideline to the copyright issue on Pinterest. Other than that, a good dose of common sense and respectful courtesy rules the day. Take a deep breath; here we go.

Pinterest bills itself as a place "to organize and share all the beautiful things you find on the web." Indeed, Pinterest is a visually stunning place filled with all manner of eye-pleasing images. But who owns these beautiful pictures? Pinterest doesn't claim ownership rights to pinned content. The terms and conditions of the user agreement grant Pinterest broad rights on the use of pinned content, but signing a user agreement doesn't consign image ownership rights to the site.

Many other social media outlets (with the exception of Google+) have very similar user agreements, which essentially license the site to "use, display, reproduce, repin, modify [e.g., reformat], rearrange, and distribute for the purposes of operating and providing service(s) to you and to our other users." The terms also state that this privilege is "royalty-free, transferable, [and] sublicensable." In other words, Pinterest users agree to permit the site to appropriate user content for free, even if he or she owns the original work's copyright. Of course, if you feel that your copyright is being violated, you can file a complaint with Pinterest. They will investigate your claim, and, if your intellectual property has been violated, the content will be taken down.

This, in turn, leads to another dilemma: The vast majority of images shared on Pinterest don't belong to the individual who pins them. Most users pin images that they find online, either through a search engine, a blog, or someone else's website. In fact, users are discouraged from engaging in excessive self-promotion. This means that if you are a painter, it is OK to pin images of your own work, but to do so exclusively is not in line with Pinterest's stated mission and suggested etiquette.

Pinterest encourages its users to "be authentic" and "express their true selves," as opposed to drumming up a mass of followers at the expense of sharing interesting and unique images.

Pinterest prohibits the use of content that "infringes upon any third party's intellectual property rights, privacy rights, publicity rights, or other personal and proprietary rights." Pinterest also encourages its users to attribute their sources, taking care that their pins link back to the original source page and not to an image search engine or third-party site that didn't originate the content. In the past, when Pinterest was first gaining traction, users often downloaded images off the internet to their computers and then uploaded them to Pinterest, rendering it difficult to credit the original source.

The artistic community is divided over whether Pinterest is an asset or a threat to their business, and many artists see Pinterest as a violation of their copyright license to control the reproduction, use, and distribution of their creative property. Although Pinterest urges its users to link back to the original source, this practice isn't always observed, and credit is not always given to the content's creator. And unlike Google image search, the images on Pinterest aren't mere thumbnails but are full-size images, meaning that they are displayed in the same size as the original upload. Critics argue that this is a violation of fair use of copyrighted material and could possibly constitute an infringement of the market value of the original work. Adding to this, Pinterest permanently stores all images on its own servers, as opposed to caching (temporary storage) as Google does.

In response to criticism of fair use and copyright violations, Pinterest provides an opt-out code on its website that can be programmed into a copyright holder's website and will prevent images on that site from being pinned. Flickr, a photo-sharing website, has adopted the code, but also provides users with the ability to opt into being pinned. Artists can further protect themselves by including watermarks on their work with their name and copyright information.

Pinterest also has a copyright complaint form on its site that allows copyright holders to file grievances about violation of their rights within the site. Images found to be in violation of copyright are removed, allowing Pinterest to claim protection under the Digital Millennium Copyright Act (DMCA), which limits its legal liability with regard to its users' activities. Liability is only limited as long as the site maintains and tries to enforce policies that are meant to protect copyright holders from infringement by its users. From a legal standpoint, Pinterest's users are the ones who are vulnerable to copyright infringement lawsuits (per the terms of use), not the site itself.

The only way Pinterest users can truly protect themselves from copyright infringement is to pin only images of their own creation—i.e., upload photos that they took themselves. This would seem to be a bit at odds with Pinterest's stated purpose of sharing all the beautiful things from all corners of the internet. This has led critics to muse that Pinterest is tacitly encouraging users to violate copyright law while at the same time washing its hands of legal responsibility for any violations.

Pinterest's sharing capabilities have been compared to those of Napster, the notorious peer-to-peer file-sharing community that facilitated and promoted illegal downloading of copyright-protected music and other content. However, Pinterest's terms of use firmly prohibit use of the site for illegal downloading purposes. Napster's explicit purpose was illegal content share and download, while Pinterest is meant as a platform for inspiration and aspiration, not appropriation.

So far in this book we have been focusing mostly on still images, but the beauty of Pinterest is that it also allows you to pin videos, Slideshare, and screencasts. Read on to learn how to use video to build up your Pinterest following and drive more traffic.

Chapter 7

Beyond Photos to Video, Podcasts, and Screencasting

While the vast majority of Pinterest users post mostly photos, you can make your Pinterest boards more of a multimedia experience by sharing videos from YouTube and Vimeo screencasts from your desktop, presentations from SlideShare, and podcasts.

According to the Association of National Advertisers 2012 Digital and Social Media Survey, 80 percent of U.S. marketers are using viral online video marketing, via platforms like YouTube, to distribute videos designed to promote business and build brand.

TEN TYPES OF VIDEOS TO PIN

Since YouTube and Vimeo have been invited to jump on the Pinterest bandwagon, you can now easily and quickly pin videos you have uploaded to either site by using the "Pin It" button from your browser or the "Add A Pin" feature on the Pinterest site in the same way you would to upload photos or other static images. A well-rounded collection of the ten types of video pins that work best for business includes:

1. Tutorials and How-to Content

There are a variety of easy-to-use, low-cost tools that allow you to practice screencasting right from your computer desktop. According to Wikipedia,

"A screencast is a digital recording of computer screen output, also known as a video screen capture, often containing audio narration." Tools such as ScreenFlow (for Mac), Camtasia (Mac and PC), and Screenr.com (Mac and PC) make creating "how-to" screencasts that you can post on YouTube and then pin on Pinterest a piece of cake.

The video tutorials and how-to content you pin need not be of your creation solely. Pinning other people's videos from YouTube or Vimeo—as long as they fit with your brand and topic—adds value to your boards.

2. Live FAQ Discussion with Staff

Instead of just posting a static list of FAQs on your website, why not present them in a more dynamic and interesting way by videotaping yourself or a staff member proffering the answers?

3. Demonstrations of How Your Product Works

Is there an aspect of your business that lends itself to product demonstration? If so, pick up your iPhone or digital SLR camera and shoot away. For example, if you are a restaurant owner, chef, or food blogger, create a video showing how to make a certain dish or apply a specific cooking technique.

4. Product Reviews

In addition to your own products, what other products might your audience be interested in seeing reviewed? You can create videos and share your opinions, tips, and

PIN WITH AN EMBEDDED LINK FROM YOUTUBE

If you plan on pinning a video from your YouTube account via its dedicated URL, you need to use the long link option provided by YouTube rather than the short link. Go to YouTube, and just below the video you want to pin is the "Share" button. Click on it, and a drop-down box will appear with a link. This is the short link, and Pinterest will reject it as spam. Instead, click the "Options" feature and check the box marked "Long Link." The long link will then appear in the drop-down box. Copy and paste this link into the "Add A Pin" feature on Pinterest to pin the image and video directly from YouTube.

evaluations about the latest and greatest in your industry; be one of the first to try out and review a new product or service; or even test unreleased products that you can video-blog about once they become available.

5. Behind-the-Scenes Tours

While researching this book, I spent countless hours perusing video picture pins, and I was surprised at how few companies take advantage of doing behind-the-scenes videos. One that is, and doing it well, is Greek furniture-maker Morphos Factory (http://pinterest.com/pin/15340454951191767/). They have managed to take something not particularly sexy—making a sofa—and, by adding music, excellent editing, and lighting, turn it into a brand enhancer. My only complaint is that the photo, which gets automatically pinned, is not a particularly pretty or engaging one, and the video is a bit long. But hey, a sofa was not made in a day.

6. Excerpts from Live Presentations and Webinars

The next time you give a speech, training, workshop, webinar, or presentation, record and then pin it. This provides potential clients with a small sampling of what you do and how you do it. In addition, you can encourage people who have attended a presentation or workshop to visit your Pinterest and see supplemental videos, or review the presentation itself, on your site.

7. Customer Testimonials and Interviews

The written customer testimonial—a staple of most websites—works even better as a live video. The two most common forms for video testimonials are dialog and monologue.

Monologue-Style Videos

Simply set up a camera and ask your client to wax poetic about the marvels of your product and service. Edit the piece down to a plucky 30 to 60 seconds, and post.

Dialog-Style Videos

If you want to create a more engaging customer testimonial video, make it an interview-style dialog, so your subject has a chance to show their spontaneous responses (i.e., agreement, enthusiasm) to questions. You need a competent interviewer—a representative of your company or an outside professional—and a series of questions developed in advance. Review the questions with your client before taping so you can make minor adjustments to their answers. But don't rehearse to such a degree that you lose the spur-of-the-moment quality that is the hallmark of good dialog-style videos.

SEARCH AND BROWSE VIDEOS TO REPIN

Don't forget that in addition to creating original videos, Pinterest also enables you to repin other pinners' videos. To browse for videos, go to the Pinterest homepage and click on the "Categories" tab at the top of the screen and then select "Videos" from the list that pops up. An entire selection of videos already pinned will pop up, and you can surf away until you find something you find pinworthy for one of your boards (see the figure below).

To search by title, put the keywords/topic you are looking for followed by the word "videos" into the Pinterest search box. For example: If you put "Makeup Videos" into the search box, it returns an entire page of videos that contain that specific keyword phrase. One downside is that you can't search by categories, only specific phrases; hence, only those videos that contain the exact words entered in the search will appear.

Yet a third option is to search for videos from pinners you follow, since you know that their topics are already in alignment with your audience and message.

Search Videos to Repin

A PAGE OF INTERVIEWS

Direct Marketing News (http://pinterest.com/directmktgnews/video/) has created an entire board composed of 101 interview videos featuring industry experts. For example, in one short, one-minute-48-second video two attendees from a recent Direct Marketing Association Conference answer the question, "What excites you most about direct marketing right now?"

Video Interviews at a Direct Marketing Association Conference

Ask the interviewee to personalize the video by clearly making a connection between their story and your product or service.

8. *Expert Interviews*

Similar in format to customer interviews, expert interviews feature a person of prominence in your field or industry talking about a topic that your audience is interested in. A talking-head-style video featuring a really smart person is far less interesting than a Q&A-style conversation between an interviewer and that same really smart person, so go for a dialog-style video whenever possible.

9. Before-and-After Stories

On reality TV and talk shows, the payoff for makeover episodes comes when the "reveal" happens. That's the time when we get to see the person, place, or thing transform from its prior form and take on a new, improved life. For example, I'm a huge fan of TLC's *What Not to Wear* (FYI, their Pinterest is http://pinterest.com/tlc/what-not-to-wear/), where hosts Stacy and Clinton take formerly bad dressers and, over the course of an hour-long TV show, turn them into stylish moms on the go and savvy-looking businesswomen. In this same way, if your product or service lends itself to a visible and/or compelling transformation, before-and-after stories may be a perfect fit for a video pin.

10. Videos That Demonstrate Your Expertise

It's no secret that people come to the internet seeking information, so video pins that highlight your specific expertise are a smart play. What do you have to share that is both hard to imitate and includes information that is in demand? Brainstorm possible ideas and, once you know what you want to say, follow these tips for creating and pinning a video that demonstrates your expertise.

Write and Rehearse a Script

Before you hit the record button, write a script and rehearse what you are going to say. While you may think you can improvise on the spot, video experts will tell you that free-flowing, extemporaneous speaking is harder than it sounds—no matter how well you know your topic. You don't have to memorize the script word for word—remember, you want to sound natural—but be sure to plan what you are going to say and practice it a few times. Keep the rhythm conversational and engaging, as you would when talking to friends.

Set the Stage

Once the camera is rolling, set the stage by introducing yourself and your organization and then frame up the video as an answer to a question you know your audience has. For example, you can say, "People are always asking me about X, and in this video, I'm going to show you the three steps to X." One way to engage the viewer is to hit them with your strongest sound bite right off the bat. Don't bury your best content 30 or 45 seconds in; instead, bring it in the first 10 seconds or risk losing the viewer.

Use Lay Language

Deliver your message using short, powerful sentences. Avoid using too many words or jargon-filled, complicated language. To keep the momentum going, illustrate your point step by step, and don't get bogged down in delivering unnecessary details.

Keep It Short

In an age where entire novels are being written one 140-character tweet at a time, it's an understatement to say that people's attention spans are drastically short. So your expert video should be between one and two minutes long. Any shorter, and you risk delivering an incomplete message; any longer, and you risk losing the viewer's attention. If you are trying to introduce something that you think will take longer than two to three minutes, imagine how you can break it down into a series of shorter videos. Video hosting company Wistia (http://wistia.com/blog) conducted an experiment and found that videos of 30 seconds or under were watched in their entirety by almost 90 percent of viewers. However, only slightly more than 50 percent of viewers made it to the end of videos that were two minutes long.

Put Your Personality into It

An endless amount of content is on the web, competing for eyeballs, so getting your videos noticed requires that they be both informative and entertaining. Even if you have great information to deliver, the video will fall flat if you don't inject your own personality into the content. Make every segment count by providing new, interesting, and engaging information from frame to frame. Repetition, vagueness, hype, and plain old boring will encourage visitors to hit the stop button and opt out of watching the rest of the video. Videos are about promoting your brand, not about the hard sell.

SHOOT SMART

Given the vast amount of amateur video on the internet today, no one is expecting yours to have the style of a Spielberg film; however, the quality of the video you post will reflect on your brand. Whether you are using your smartphone, a digital SLR, a video camera, or a webcam, there are a few steps you can take to ensure that your videos come out on the spiffy side.

I'm married to an award-winning video content strategist and producer, so I asked him for a few of his best tips on making engaging videos. Jon Leland is president of ComBridges (http://combridges.com) and an avid Pinterest fan (http://pinterest.com/joncombridges/). Here's his two cents:

Choose the Right Equipment

There is no shortage of relatively inexpensive cameras that you can use to make your own media. Some of the best rated include:

- Panasonic Lumix DMC-LX5
- Canon PowerShot SX260 HS Digital Camera

- Nikon Coolpix P7100
- Sony Cyber-shot DSC-HX100V

In addition, smartphones have created a whole slew of videographers who shoot and edit entire videos all in the palm of their hands. Beyond a camera, the other useful accouterments you need include:

An External Microphone

"The most common mistake amateurs make in shooting effective video is the quality of the sound," says Leland. "Using the speaker on your computer or smartphone is insufficient and produces a video where you can't be well heard, and background noise is often at the forefront."

Leland suggests using an external microphone. For webcam videos (videos shot via your computer desktop), a simple USB microphone, such as one from Audio-Technica (AT2020 model) or Blue Microphones, is a good place to start.

Likewise, if you plan on shooting video with a digital SLR, buy one that has an external microphone jack built in. Leland says Rode and Sennheiser make good external mics for camera use.

A Tripod

Smartphones, digital cameras, and even video cameras today are so compact and light that they tend to have stabilization problems and easily shake when hand held. One way to give your video an instant upgrade is to use a tripod. For shooting with a smartphone, Leland recommends the Gorilla Pod, which enables you to mount your smartphone almost anywhere.

Get Good Lighting

Engaging video, be it on the web or your TV screen, almost always has good lighting. "The thing to watch out for is backlighting," says Leland. "Your primary light source needs to be in front of the subject." For example, the worst-case scenario is where you seat yourself or your subject with a window or bright light source behind you or it. "It makes all the difference in the world to face the subject toward the camera and the light," says Leland.

Go for Close-ups

Just as "filling the frame with the focal point" is optimal when taking photos for Pinterest, close-ups work best for videos. The framing you choose should be shot close enough to show viewers the details that will make the piece engaging. "The essence of video engagement is the expression of your or your subject's authentic voice," says Leland. "So if you want your viewers to connect with you in a more intimate way, they need to be able to see and hear you up close and personal."

Edit Your Footage

With the plethora of editing software available on the market today, editing your video is easier than ever. For a low-priced option, both iMovie and Windows Movie Maker work well. However, if you want to use a more sophisticated piece of software, Leland suggests going for Final Cut Pro for Mac or Avid Premier Pro for PC or Mac. Just be warned that more advanced video editing software requires more processing power and has a steeper learning curve.

POST THOUGHTFULLY, BRAND CAREFULLY, AND TRACK RESULTS

As with all Pinterest content, your goal is to be an active presence, not an annoyance. Try to provide a steady stream of video content, as opposed to dumping a bunch of video pins all at once; keep your brand front and center in the videos you pin; and track the results as you go along. You want to know which types of videos are most effective, so check for increased spikes in traffic to your website when you post a new video, and with Pinterest itself to see who is liking, repinning, or commenting on video you have pinned. To make the most of your video pins:

- *Keep your brand consistent.* If your brand has an established visual element, such as a logo, make sure to include it in the video. You can begin and end the video with it, or keep it visible in the lower third of the screen throughout the video.
- *Provide a call to action.* At the end of the video, provide the viewer with next steps, such as asking them to share the video, pin the video, or subscribe to your mailing list for additional content. For example: "If you liked this video about how to negotiate a raise, please pin it"; or, "For more tips on rocking your workplace, sign up for our mailing list at (your website)." Be sure to include your URL at the bottom of the screen.
- *Add a clickable link.* Don't forget to add clickable links to all your videos. Live links embedded in your videos are accessible by a visitor playing your presentation and give you the opportunity to have viewers click through to your website, blog posts, or designated landing pages from within Pinterest and the video they are watching.
- *Optimize your video with keywords.* In the same way that you optimize your blog posts with keywords, you want to optimize your video pins. Use the keywords or

phrases that your audience searches for as your video title. For example, I have an excerpt from a keynote speech I did for entrepreneurs on personal branding, so I named the video on YouTube "Personal Branding" and then posted it on a Pinterest board that I named—you guessed it—"Personal Branding." Since I know that this is a keyword often searched by my audience of senior executives and high-end entrepreneurs, I've made it the title of my video and pin to make it easily searchable. Don't get overly clever or abstract with the title, which risks obscuring your content in the Pinterest search engine. It doesn't matter how great your video is if no one can find it in a search.

YOUTUBE ON PINTEREST

Besides being able to pin videos you post (or find) on YouTube, the media mogul itself has a very active Pinterest site (http://pinterest.com/YouTube/) with more than 15,000 followers.

According to YouTube's official blog, they have "brought together a Pinterest dream team at YouTube to share videos we hope you'll find particularly useful, informative, and inspiring—with a goal that every video we share will 'wow' you."

This move is a way for YouTube to curate and share content in a more streamlined way. According to YouTube's FAQ, 48 hours of video are uploaded to the main site every minute, resulting in almost eight years of content placed on the site daily.

The categories of boards that YouTube presents on its Pinterest page align with the most popular categories on Pinterest and can be a great source of video repins. Specific boards include:

- *Life Hacking.* A how-to board showing everything from how to fix broken sunglasses to how to clean up broken glass with a slice of bread.

- *Go, Go, Go.* Features videos from users' travels and adventures around the world.

- *Nom, Nom, Nom.* For all you foodies out there, these are recipes à la video including everything from a sweet potato French fry recipe from the White House kitchen to spicy Indian lemonade.

- *Pinspirational.* All manner of videos that uplift, inspire, and motivate.

SET UP YOUR VIDEO TO DRIVE TRAFFIC BACK TO YOUR SITE

Whenever you pin a video directly from YouTube or Vimeo, the pin is designated on Pinterest with a white "play" arrow in the middle of the image.

When a user presses the arrow, the video immediately pops up and plays (via YouTube), but the user doesn't leave Pinterest. So while this gives your audience a video to watch, it does nothing to help drive traffic back to your site. To seamlessly direct the video back to your website, but still use it as a pin, do the following:

- First, be sure that the video you want to feature is embedded somewhere on your website—on your blog, homepage, or a dedicated page of videos—even if it's hosted on YouTube.
- Next, download a screen capture tool, such as Skitch (Mac) or Jing (Mac, Windows), so that you can grab a screen shot of your video to use as a pin.
- Go to the video you want to pin and, using the tool, grab the video image (with the white play arrow)—that will be your pin—and drag it to your computer desktop.
- To place this image as a pin, follow the process for adding a pin via the "Upload a Pin" option from the Pinterest site. Assign the pin a board and save it. At this point, you will have a pin featuring your video screen shot, complete with white play arrow, but it won't be live and play because it's not yet linked to the video on your site. To complete this final, critical step, do the following: Hover your cursor over the video image in Pinterest and click on the "Edit" button at the top of the image. It will open up to a dialog box. Enter a description of the pin and, in the box below where it says "Link," enter the dedicated URL of the page where the video is housed on your website. This will link the pinned image of the video to the page where the video plays on YouTube. Save the changes to the pin and, *voilà*, users can now click on the white arrow and be taken to your website, where they can watch the video—and, while there, learn more about your business and brand.

PIN SLIDESHARE PRESENTATIONS

The easy integration between Pinterest and SlideShare offers you yet another way to establish an expertise in your field by curating great content. Browse SlideShare and find the presentation (your own or someone else's) that you want to pin, and click on the "Pin It" button from your browser.

Whatever presentation you pin will automatically be given attribution, and you can decide which of your boards to pin it to. You may also want to create a pinboard or boards dedicated to SlideShare-only decks—for example, those from your speaking engagements.

By pinning your presentation slides, you enable participants to review your deck after they have seen you live, and also give potential clients an inside look at what you offer.

PIN PODCASTS

The film *Joffrey Mavericks* (http://pinterest.com/joffreymovie/) has a board on its Pinterest page that features podcasts with alumni of the ballet company. Each pin is a photo of the person being interviewed. The user clicks on the image and is taken to Soundcloud.com, where the podcast lives.

Soundcloud is a perfect tool for creating podcasts to pin. The site allows you to record and upload your originally created sounds in just a few clicks and is set up to deal with all kinds of audio formats, so you can concentrate on your content, not technology.

Once you've recorded and uploaded to SoundCloud, you can then easily share and promote your sounds by connecting your account with Twitter, Facebook and, of course, pinning your podcasts.

Being a great curator of videos and still images that you pin is one important way to participate on Pinterest. The other is to make your website Pinterest friendly, so that fellow pinners who visit your site can pin with ease.

Make Your Website Pinterest Friendly

With hoards of businesses clamoring to fill their Pinterest boards with beautiful images, more people will come calling online to find great visuals to pin, and optimizing your website for Pinterest can drive traffic to your site. Here's how:

GIVE EVERY PAGE AND POST A FEATURED IMAGE

For someone to pin a page from your website, or a post from your blog, it must have an accompanying image. This means placing an image you would want someone to pin on the important pages of your website and giving each blog post you write a photo to go with it.

Don't disregard your older posts. Pinterest knows no timeline, so a blog post you wrote two years ago may still resonate deeply with the Pinterest community—but if it has no image with it, it won't get pinned. Go back to older posts that are either imageless or have pictures that aren't up to par, and give them a visual overhaul. For specifics on where to find great images, check out the recommendations in Chapter 5.

MEET MINIMUM SIZE REQUIREMENTS

To optimize your website images for Pinterest, make sure they are at least 250 pixels on both sides. If possible, go with the maximum width allowable, which is 600 pixels—there is no limit on length.

CHECK OUT YOUR DOMAIN'S SOURCE PAGE

To see if your current images are well-optimized for Pinterest, go to http://pinterest
.com/source/YourDomain.com. Replace the words "Your Domain.com" with the
name of your actual URL domain name. Once you are there, a page pops up showing images from your page that have been pinned either by you or other people.
Clicking on each individual image will open it up to full pin size. Images that are too
small will be surrounded by gray space; go to the image on your website and adjust
their sizing.

ADD TEXT

One way to optimize your images and expand your brand is to add text to the images on
your site. Adding keywords or a URL allows the text to be automatically pinned as part
of the package.

INSTALL THE "PIN IT" BUTTON FOR WEBSITES

In Chapter 5, you learned about installing the "Pin It" button on your browser so you
can automatically pin images you find while surfing the web. The "Pin It" button for
websites allows others to automatically pin what they find on your website. Having it
visible on pages and posts acts as a prompt to encourage visitors to pin your content. A
few things to keep in mind:

- The "Pin It" button can't be universally applied; it must be manually added by
  you, or your webmaster, to each page or post of your website.
- You must identify which image you want pinned for each page or post.
- You can place the "Pin It" button at the beginning, end, or side of the content, but
  the more visible it is, the more likely it is to be used.

To install the "Pin It" button for your website, log into your Pinterest account and,
from the homepage, go to the drop-down menu under the "About" link and click on the
"Pin It" option.

Scroll down to the "Pin It Button for Websites" section. A box will appear asking you
to enter the URL for the page to be pinned. Copy the dedicated URL for that page (not
your homepage URL), and paste it into the text box (see Figure 8–1, page 89).

FIGURE 8–1. The "Pin It" Button for Blogs and Website Pages

Next, find the URL of the image associated with that page and paste it into the text box just under the one in which you placed your post-page URL. You can usually find the URL of the image by clicking on the image itself (or right-clicking) and then copying the URL that appears.

Once the page and image URLs have been entered, you can add a description of the pin. It's to your advantage to do so, since the description will appear when the image is pinned.

Finally, you can choose which "Pin It" button format you would like to appear on your webpage. Go to the "Pin Count" drop-down menu on the far right and select one of the following:

■ A horizontal "Pin It" button, which also displays the number of times that a particular page or image has been pinned.

■ A vertical "Pin It" button, which also displays the number of times that a particular page or image has been pinned.

■ No Count. A plain, horizontal "Pin It" button, with no associated pin count.

With your choices made, a code will appear at the bottom of the box with instructions on how to copy and paste to your web page, based on where you want the button to appear.

USE A WORDPRESS PLUGIN

If your website or blog is in WordPress, you are in luck since you have the option of using a WordPress plugin to add the "Pin It" button to your site. Two of the most highly recommended can be found at:

www.wordpress.org/extend/plugins/pinterest-pin-it-button/

www.pinterestplugin.com

To see a full list of all the WordPress plugins available for Pinterest, go to www. Wordpress.org/extend/plugins/search.php?p=pinterest. Enter the word "Pinterest" into the text box, and then click "Search Plugins." A page of options will appear, complete with ratings and reviews. From here you can choose the plugin that fits the best.

Two other recommended WordPress plugins for optimizing your website for Pinterest are:

- *The Pinterest RSS WordPress Widget.* This lets you showcase thumbnail images of your most recent pins on your website sidebar. Each one has a direct link to the individual pin's URL, which encourages viewers to check out your Pinterest page. As a bonus, you can choose which of four different sizes of "Follow Me On Pinterest" buttons will show up at the bottom of your list of pins. The widget can be found at www.Wordpress.org/extend/plugins/pinterest-rss-widget.

OPTING OUT

Pinterest has a small bit of code available if you don't want the images from your website available for pinning. Anyone who tries to pin an image will see a message explaining that your site doesn't allow it. To find the code, follow these steps:

Go to http://pinterest.com/about/help/ and, close to the bottom, find the bold heading "Linking to your blog or website." Under this, click on the subhead titled: "What if I don't want images from my site to be pinned?" You will then see a piece of code that your webmaster can copy and paste on the head of any page on your website.

Keep in mind that this doesn't prevent Pinterest users from taking screenshots or downloading images by right-clicking and choosing "Save As." In reality, they could do either of these things and then re-upload the images to Pinterest—one reason why it's crucial to watermark your original images.

■ *WP Pinner*. This tool lets you automatically pin your blog posts—including selecting images for each post and which board you want to pin it to—and add a description to the pin. The plugin also shows you how many click-throughs your pinned WordPress posts receive, as well as the number of likes and repins, which makes this a nice little analytics tool as well (you'll learn all about analytics and tracking in Chapter 16). You can find the free widget at www.wppinner.com.

PUT UP A "FOLLOW ME ON PINTEREST" BUTTON

In the same way that you encourage visitors to join your other social media sites (LinkedIn, Facebook, and Twitter) by placing a click-through button on your website, you can advertise with a "Follow Me on Pinterest" button (see Figure 8–2). Ready-to-roll buttons can be found at Pinterest at http://pinterest.com/about/goodies/. Place this on either the top or side of your website and always "above the fold," which renders it visible without the viewer having to scroll down the page.

FIGURE 8–2. The "Follow Me On Pinterest" Button

Congratulations! By this point, you've made it through the sign-up, strategy, and setup of Pinterest. Next, we need to get you out there finding people to follow and creating followers of your own.

Follow and
Be Followed

One of the fundamental underpinnings of all social media sites is striking that delicate balance between finding people you want to follow and building up a cadre of people who want to follow you. Pinterest is no exception. An ongoing challenge facing users is figuring out a Pinterest-friendly strategy.

The goal with Pinterest—as with any social media—is to be a connector, not a collector. This means choosing thoughtfully whom you want to follow based on your overall brand strategy and marketing goals. For example, if you're a real estate company, pinners in these categories might make good candidates for you to follow:

- Top-of-the-line real estate experts or advisors
- Real estate publications or magazines
- Well-known home decorators, designers, or architects
- Real estate industry leaders
- Mortgage brokers and banks
- Contractors

Who wouldn't make sense—or be off-brand—might include race-car drivers, an online lingerie shop, a chocolatier, and a travel agency. While these might be personal interests of yours, following too many boards based on these topics would dilute your business brand.

FINDING PEOPLE AND BRANDS TO FOLLOW

As social media goes, Pinterest is a relatively new player—but growing by leaps and bounds. In 2012 it hit the comScore (http://www.comscore.com) list of the top 50 most visited websites in the United States and is, at the time of this writing, the third-largest referral source for traffic to a website, after Facebook and Twitter.

So, if your clients, friends, and business associates aren't already on Pinterest, chances are they will be soon, and this allows you to follow them—and hopefully have them follow you back. Your homepage is where the pins (and repins) of the people you follow show up, so curate carefully the players whose pins you want to see on a regular basis. Here are the basics:

Pinterest Gives You a Head Start

When you set up your profile way back in Chapter 2, Pinterest inquired about your interests and automatically set you up to begin following some of the top people in those categories. They are a good starter set, and you can unfollow them at any time. Users aren't notified when someone unfollows them, so no need to worry about causing offense.

You Can Follow People or Boards

When you "follow" a person on Pinterest, all of the boards that they create will show up in the feed on your main Pinterest page. Alternatively, you can also choose to follow only certain individual boards that pinner has created. When you take this option, you won't see pins from all of an individual's boards in your feed, just those from the board(s) you selected to follow.

For example, let's say user Patsy Pinner has an individual board called "Interesting Industrial Machinery" that you are fascinated by and can't wait to follow. However, her other boards ("Pretty Kites" and "Killer High Heels") are leaving you flat. You can choose to follow just the "Industrial Machinery" board and skip the others. If you are enthralled with all Patsy's boards, you can follow her as a person, and all her pins will show up in your Pinterest feed stream.

Locate Facebook Friends on Pinterest

If your Pinterest account is linked to your Facebook, you will be able to see all of your Facebook friends who are on Pinterest. Log in to your Pinterest account and hover your cursor over your name in the upper right side of your screen. When the drop-down menu appears, select "Find Friends" and then click on the "Facebook" tab. If you selected the option in settings of connecting Pinterest to your Facebook account, you will see a list of your Facebook friends who have joined Pinterest in the right-hand column.

Browse through your Facebook friends on Pinterest, and select the ones you want by clicking on the "Follow" button next to each individual's name. Remember that by doing so, you are choosing to follow the person—and hence all of their boards—not just an individual board or two that they have created. In the left-hand column is a list of Facebook friends without Pinterest accounts. You can click "Invite" next to a person's name to send them a Pinterest invitation via Facebook.

Using Pinterest Search to Find People and Businesses to Follow

Another way to find people (or businesses) you want to follow but aren't connected to you on Facebook, is to conduct a straight search.

Log into Pinterest and locate the search bar in the top left-hand corner of the screen. Enter the name of the person or business you're looking for—e.g., Michelle Obama, Banana Republic, *The New York Times*—and hit "Enter" or click the magnifying glass icon next to the text box. The search results will display all of the pins that contain that name on screen.

An option directly under the search box will appear that allows you to refine the search by focusing on the name you entered for either "Pins," "Boards," or "Pinners." Select the "Pinners" link to filter out all other results. Since Pinterest treats companies and brands as people, always click on the "Pinners" link, even to find a business. Keep in mind that you may get several profiles back and need to open each one to determine which is the one you want.

For example, if you enter *"The New York Times"* into the search bar and then narrow the search to "Pinners" (designated in red), this means you are asking Pinterest to find any company, person, or brand whose profile name is *The New York Times*—not individual pins or boards with that name.

As you can see, several options come up. If it's not immediately obvious which is the one you want, click on "Pin" itself to open up to that pinner's page and find exactly who you are looking for. Once you find the person or business you want to follow, click on the red "Follow All" button beneath their profile picture to follow all of their boards.

Alternatively, you can view their boards individually and click the red "Follow" button, located directly beneath the board name, to follow just those boards you are interested in. For example, *The New York Times* has a board named "Restaurant Picks, New York." If you wanted to just follow that individual board, you have that option. There's no limit to how many individual boards you can follow from any given pinner, so pick and choose based on what interests you or would be most useful to you for repin purposes.

UNFOLLOWING PEOPLE AND BOARDS

As mentioned earlier in this chapter, following a fellow pinner is not a life sentence, and you are free to unfollow at any point.

To unfollow an individual, navigate to your main Pinterest page. Below your profile picture and brief bio is a secondary menu bar. At the far right of the bar, Pinterest shows you how many followers you have and how many people you are following. Click on the "Following" link, and you will see all the users (with their photos) that you are following.

Next to everyone's name is an "Unfollow" button, which looks grayed out. Click it, and the button darkens and changes to say "Follow" next to that person's name. This way, if you change your mind in the future, you can again follow your friend. There is no limit on how many times you can follow and unfollow a person or their boards, and they don't get notified. So, if you're the fickle type, not to worry.

If you want to unfollow certain boards, follow the same procedure to get to your followers, but click on the individual's name to view all of their boards. You can then choose to unfollow certain boards by clicking the "Unfollow" button located under each board.

Use Google Search to Find People to Follow

Another easy way to find specific people or companies you want to follow on Pinterest is to do a Google search with the person or company name followed by the word "Pinterest." For example, you could enter the words "wall street journal pinterest" into the Google search box, and you would be rewarded with http://pinterest.com/wsj/, which, upon clicking, would take you directly to the *WSJ* profile page.

Follow People Besides Your Friends

Yes, you are interested in the things your friends are pinning, but part of the fun and business opportunity of Pinterest is finding and following interesting pins from people you've never met. This can lead to discovering exciting new content related to your brand and business. The following are a few ways to locate nonfriends.

Check Out Pinpuff.com

This site measures Pinterest sway on a 100-point scale and considers 50 or above an influential user. In addition to discovering your own rating on the site, you can use the "Random User" button to discover new pinners with high scores. There's also a tab called "Interests" with a drop-down menu of categories (i.e., food, travel, lifestyle) that pulls up three popular pinners in that category.

Surf the Site

To find people to follow while browsing, hover your cursor over the pin and locate the name of the pinner below the image.

Click on the person's name, and you will be taken to a page featuring all their boards. Above their boards is a red "Follow All" button. Select this button to follow this individual pinner. When you do, all of their pins (from all of their boards) will show up in your main Pinterest feed. Alternatively, you may choose to follow only certain boards by that pinner by clicking on the board name and then selecting the red "Follow" button for that board.

Browse by Keywords

The categories in Pinterest are fairly broad, so to find pinners you may want to follow, it's better to narrow the search down to a specific topic and/or keyword. Using the search bar, located in the upper left-hand corner of the screen, type the keyword you're looking for and press "Enter" or click on the magnifying glass next to the search box. The results page will feature the pins, boards, and pinners most relevant to your keyword search.

Find Pinners to Follow through Reverse Engineering

If you see a pin or board that catches your attention, you can find the name of the person who posted it directly below the image. Click through and check out their boards to see if they are someone you may want to follow. Be sure to see if there is a "via" in the posting credits. This means that the image you are looking at was originally posted by the pinner whose name follows the "via." In this case, check out that person's boards as well.

Give Everything a Glance

The default when you log into Pinterest is that only pins from those boards/pinners you are following show up in your stream. One source of new pinners to follow is the "Everything" link, located at the top of your menu bar. Clicking this tab brings up a Mr. Toad's Wild Ride of pins, giving you the opportunity to stumble across some fabulous new pinner you've probably never heard of and may want to follow.

BUILDING UP YOUR PINTEREST FOLLOWING

If you do nothing else but follow the recommendations in this book—i.e., optimize your pins and website, find great people to follow, use keywords in your descriptions, etc.—you will organically build an audience on Pinterest.

One word of caution: Before you begin a campaign to get more followers, get your Pinterest house in order. In other words, make sure your boards and profile are ready for public viewing. If you reach out to potential followers, and they come to your page only to find that you have nothing up—or nothing worthwhile—you're not likely to get a second chance.

Beyond that bottom-line advice, if you are looking to be highly proactive in increasing your Pinterest following, here are some strategies to consider.

Build More Niched Boards

Take a look at the most popular players on Pinterest, and it will become immediately clear that they have a plethora of boards, usually between 50 and 100, on average. It's also obvious that those same power users have gone to great efforts to make their boards as niched as possible so that they stand a better chance of being found (and followed) by a targeted audience. For example, if you're a cookbook writer, a single board named "desserts" that features all manner of sugary goodies would work, but you might draw more followers if you took that same board and split it into four—one each for:

- Pies and cakes
- Cookies and bars
- Chocolate
- Ice creams, sorbets, and puddings

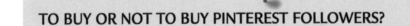

TO BUY OR NOT TO BUY PINTEREST FOLLOWERS?

When you start out on Pinterest you will, as expected, have very few followers. Some businesses believe the best way to address this problem is to purchase followers by hiring a company that offers to deliver them for a price. For example, if you Google "purchase Pinterest followers," a whole slew of providers comes up that promises "500 followers delivered in 3 days for $50.00," and such.

TO BUY OR NOT TO BUY PINTEREST FOLLOWERS?, CONTINUED

This is a topic of serious debate among social media pundits and practitioners. Opinions on this topic vary, but the vast majority of experts I spoke with weighed in with a resounding "NO." I have to say, I agree. Social media is at its heart about connection, not collection. Buying followers or repins may seem like a way to game the system, but ultimately, it doesn't achieve the quality of followers that makes a Pinterest site truly satisfying or successful. Here's what a couple of my fellow marketing brethren had to say.

"Buying followers on Pinterest will follow the same path as similar ideas for blogs, Facebook, and Twitter into the dustbin of digital history. There is temptation to take this step, as marketers have been trained for decades to buy audiences with mass media dollars, and they often wish to quickly boost their follower base soon after launching Pinterest accounts. However, most marketers know by now that these 'purchased' followers offer little real value in the long run. Paid followers have little interest in the brands themselves. No wonder that large companies such as Procter & Gamble have enacted company policies against using such services. Social has been and will always be about earning customer attention and sales by adding value."

—Bob Gilbreath (http://twitter.com/mktgwithmeaning), author of
The Next Evolution of Marketing: Connect with Your Customers by Marketing with Meaning
(McGraw-Hill, 2009)

"Buying fans and followers is an unethical practice. Social media marketing is inherently organic and cannot be treated the same as traditional marketing channels. The goal is not to push your message out to an audience who may or may not be interested—circa 1960s, Mad Men-style. It's to build a genuine community who clamors for (well, at least has clearly expressed interest in) the information or services you offer. The companies that excel at social media understand that this takes time and creativity and cannot be bought. It is a natural derivative of showcasing your company culture, consistently providing value, and nurturing relationships over time. It isn't easy, instant, or free (strategies take time and money). But it is certainly worth doing correctly."

—Shama Kabani (www.MarketingZen.com), bestselling author of
The Zen of Social Media Marketing (BenBella Books, 2012)

By refining your boards to be more relevant to the people who are the most interested in those specific topics, or aspects of a topic, you increase your chances of getting followers.

Mega-retailer Bloomingdales (http://pinterest.com/bloomingdales/) is doing a great job of this. They have more than 25,000 followers and 58 boards, many of which are nicely niched. For example, they have a "Good As Gold" board, featuring all gold-tone items from nail polish to purses; a "Sneakers" board, starring a sneaker wardrobe; and their "Rain With Style!" board, which showcases all rain-oriented fashion items, including umbrellas, boots, and trench coats.

Another example of niched boards comes from Ahalife (http://pinterest.com/ahalife/), which sells unique gift items curated from around the world.

"Our whole goal when we create a board is not to sell our products, but to make it engaging enough that people will want to repin the images," says Ahalife founder Shauna Mei. For example, one of Ahalife's niched boards is "Witty Workspaces" that showcases offices using creative and intelligent design.

As for the results, Mei says that the bounce rate is much lower for customers who come to Ahalife.com from Pinterest and they tend to spend an average of 50 percent longer lingering on the website.

Pin Your Passions

Nothing is more engaging than a pinner who is passionate about his or her topic(s). Even if one or more of your boards is not directly related to what your business or brand does, a particular passion for your nonbusiness-related hobbies, interests, goals, and dreams can get you followers. Those same followers may at some point become so interested in who you are that they begin to pay attention to what you have to offer in the business sphere.

Even straight business/brand accounts on Pinterest would do well to have a board or two that brings the personal into the mix. For example, show your staff at a company picnic, highlight a particular hobby you, as the small-business owner, have, or create a board of fun, wacky, crazy things that relate to your company or brand.

Take Timing into Consideration

As with all social media sites, timing does play a factor in finding followers. According to research by Reachli.com (www.reachli.com), the best times to pin are between 2 and 4 P.M., and 8 P.M. and 1 A.M., EST. In addition, Bitly.com reports that Saturday morning is an optimal time to post.

Jump on the Trending Topics Bandwagon

People, places, and events that are in the now and popular at the moment make great bait for finding new followers. Topics that are trending hot will be getting keyword-searched on the site, and if you have a pin that fits and is properly hashtagged, you stand a good chance of picking up some of that traffic. Reachli.com says that pins related to trending topics see an average of a 94 percent increase in click-throughs. So it pays to pay attention, not only to the trending topics on Pinterest but also to what's trending on other social media sites. A few great resources include:

- http://trendsmap.com/ provides a real-time mapping of Twitter trends across the world
- http://www.google.com/trends/hottrends shows the current hot searches in the United States

Practice Newsjacking

Related to the idea of trending topics, newsjacking is a term coined by marketing guru David Meerman Scott that refers to the act of appropriating a news story to increase recognition of your business or brand.

One word of caution: Newsjacking is a delicate business when it comes to natural disasters, wars, and other events where people suffer significant hardship and loss. For example, when Hurricane Sandy hit the Eastern Seaboard in late 2012, entrepreneur Neel Patel created a board titled "Hurricane Hair" (http://pinterest.com/debonaire/hurricane-hair/), spotlighting beautiful people with wind-tossed locks. As users searched for hurricane-related pins, his boards gained traffic. Patel's approach to newsjacking was light-spirited and had no ill intentions, but it still garnered serious controversy and heated debate in the blogosphere.

If you are going to practice newsjacking via Pinterest, I suggest the following guidelines for any related boards and pins you create.

Provide Useful Information

Create a board that is a resource for citizens on the facts of the situation, status updates, and helpful ideas. For example, if a natural disaster strikes, a company such as REI (http://pinterest.com/reicoop/), which sells outdoor gear and clothing, could have created a board featuring the ten essential things to have on hand in case of flood or fire: waterproof matches, a battery-operated lantern, water filtration bottles, etc.

Offer Messages of Hope, Inspiration, Insight, and Empathy

Snarkiness may sell, but is that really what you want your brand associated with, especially in the face of suffering? Take the tasteful approach and pin images and quotes that uplift those affected.

Use Your Popularity to Galvanize Action

If your brand has a large following on Pinterest, create a board that features various ways people can make a difference. For example, pin charities and places where people can contribute or make a donation to a particular cause or situation.

Use Humor Sparingly

Newsjacking that involves celebrity gossip, nondisaster national or world events, or seasonal stories provides you with a bit more leeway to pin with a bit of tongue and cheek. However, good taste and plain old manners should still be what guide you. Remember: Famous, rich, thin, and beautiful movie stars are people, too.

Post to Your Most Popular Boards

Obvious? Yes. Often practiced? No. For those boards of yours that have a significantly larger following than others, post with slightly more frequency. Since more people are following these boards, your chances for a higher rate of repins—and hence new followers—is greater. For more details, see Chapter 16 on tracking your performance.

26,000 FOLLOWERS IN THREE DAYS

Consider the case of Andrew "Oyl" Miller, who went from 250 Pinterest followers to 26,000—in just three days. Today, he boasts a Pinterest following of 1.4 million. What was Miller's journey? Here's what he had to say:

Q. *When did you join Pinterest?*

A. I signed up for Pinterest the week it launched. I had been a faithful Tumblr user and was intrigued by the visual nature of Pinterest. I also saw some professional benefits of the platform as it related to my day job as a creative at Wieden+Kennedy (an advertising agency). I set up some boards, learned how it worked, but didn't really get hooked. So I let my account gather dust and didn't use it for over a year.

Q. *What inspired you to start using it again?*

A. I started reading a lot of tech articles suddenly touting Pinterest as a possible third social networking companion to the already established Facebook and

Twitter. At this point I started to give Pinterest more attention, and be strategic about it.

Q. *Did you dive right in, or start slowly?*

A. I made a small commitment to use Pinterest every day. Each morning, after I was done going through my email, I would surf the web for 10 minutes, specifically looking for images to pin to my Pinterest profile. I would browse my favorite sports and culture blogs. I didn't have many followers at that point but was hoping to establish a great depth to my boards that would hopefully be exciting for users who happened to stumble into them.

Q. *You had a breakthrough by leveraging a world event. What was it?*

A. The 2012 London Olympic Games happened. The web was filled with inspiring photos of athletes and the various sports. I was finding a lot of great Olympic content and started pinning all the great shots I found. On the third day of the Olympics, I received an email notification that 10,000 people had just started following my Pinterest profile. I was ecstatic! Two hours later, I received another email letting me know that 2,000 more people started following me. Then I turned the notifications off. And I haven't looked back.

Q. *Your number of followers has brought you some interesting offers and contacts, yes?*

A. After one month, I had accumulated 500,000 followers. After two months, I hit 1 million. I updated my Pinterest growth to all of my social networks and started hearing back from people, companies, and brands who wondered what my secret was. I've been offered jobs at technology companies, advertising agencies, and brands based on my meteoric Pinterest rise. It has helped me connect with some very interesting and high-profile people in the creative industry. I'm looking forward to seeing what opportunities my Pinterest profile can open in the future.

Engage with the Pinterest Community

Using hashtags and the @ symbol for mentions, liking, and commenting are all great ways to build up a following. For details, see Chapter 10.

Follow High-Profile and Highly Relevant People

While the criteria for who you follow should first and foremost be the relevance of their pins to your business and brand, there's a case to be made for having at least 10 percent of who you choose be the big dogs in their fields. By following these power players, you increase the chances that they will follow you back, repin, like, and comment on your images, and in general give you greater exposure to their large followings.

Use Keywords in All Your Pins

As discussed in Chapter 6, paying attention to SEO is a significant part of pinning. The more on target you are with the keywords you use in your boards and pin descriptions, the more likely you are to draw followers searching for and interested in those topics. For more details on keyword selection, see Chapter 4.

Promote Pinterest with Your Email Newsletter

Given the stringent no-spam requirements that exist for email marketing today, it's a safe bet that the people already on your distribution list want to hear from you. Several ways to build up your Pinterest following with a newsletter include:

- Announcing your presence on the site in a regular newsletter you send and encouraging readers to click through and follow you.
- Sending out a pithy, photo-heavy announcement about your Pinterest, inspiring your tribe to find out more.
- Enticing readers to visit your Pinterest boards by placing a Pinterest icon that links through to your page on all future email newsletter communications and featuring a "hot" pin or two you've recently posted.

Most email marketing services (Constant Contact, MailChimp, etc.) provide data on click-through rates from the links posted in a newsletter. Keeping tabs on how effective your Pinterest marketing efforts are will help you pivot and change tactics as needed.

Add Pinterest to Your Email Signature Line

Talk about your low-hanging fruit. You have the opportunity with every email you send to anyone—client, potential client, friend, colleague, stranger you just met on the airplane, you name it—to promote your Pinterest and gain followers. Simply add the dedicated URL of your Pinterest to the end of your signature line, where the links to your other social media (website, Twitter, Facebook, LinkedIn) live, and allow people to follow you with a single click.

Reciprocate

If you've spent any time on Twitter, you've already cut your teeth on this dilemma, but the same protocol applies: You have no obligation to follow back everyone who follows you on Pinterest.

HOW TO FIND YOUR PINTEREST PROFILE URL

If you want to send someone directly to your Pinterest profile, you need to provide the dedicated URL to your Pinterest profile. To do this, log into Pinterest and click on your name and profile photo in the upper right-hand corner. This will open up your profile page. Locate the URL, and copy it for future reference. The standard format for a Pinterest profile URL is pinterest.com/username.

○ ○ ○		
📇 **Karen Leland – Sterling Marketi...** ✕	📌 **Sterling Marketing Group (kare...** ✕	**＋**
◀ 🌐 **pinterest.com**/karenleland/		

Your Pinterest Profile's Dedicated URL

However, the laws of reciprocity are always at play. A good best practice is to always check out a new follower, or someone who has liked or repinned one of your images, and consider whether you want to follow them back. Some of the criteria to take into account include:

- Are they a major player in the same space? If so, consider following them, since your audiences are likely to be the same.
- Are they pinning interesting, uplifting, beautiful, or highly informative content? If yes, they are worth following as a regular resource for repinning.
- Are they someone on whose radar you would like to be? Following someone increases the chances they will follow you back and gives you regular opportunity to comment, like, and repin their images.

Now that you've gotten some people to play with you in the Pinterest sandbox, you can't just sit there doing nothing. To really make your presence on Pinterest count, and to build up your brand, you need to engage with your audience and the Pinterest community at large.

Engage with the Pinterest Community:
Liking, Hashtags, Commenting, and Tagging

While Pinning and repinning might be how most members spend their time on the site, building your brand by engaging with the community at large through other actions is equally important. There are four primary tools available for connecting and engaging with your fellow pinners, and they are: liking, commenting, hashtags, and tagging.

LIKING

Here's a common scenario: You're browsing your Pinterest feed when you come across a particular pin that strikes your fancy, but you don't necessarily want to repin it, since it may not quite fit with your brand or business. Instead you can "like" it.

Liking vs. Repinning

"Liking" on Pinterest works in much the same way as it does on Facebook—it's a nod to the pinner that what they have posted pleases you—but it's not the same as repinning. Liking a pin doesn't add the pin to any of your pinboards or make it available to view the way repinning does.

The advantage of liking is that you can see all of the pins you have marked in this way by selecting the "Likes" tab in the drop-down menu under your profile name and photo on your Pinterest homepage. This gives you the opportunity to essentially bookmark a pin and go back to repin or comment on it at a later date.

To like a pin, you need only click on the "Like" button that appears at the top of the image when you hover your cursor over the pin.

When you "like" someone's pin, they are informed of it by their news feed. Conversely, if someone "likes" one of your pins, it will appear in your news feed on your Pinterest home screen.

Like Liberally

"Liking" lets you interact with other pinners who share your interests and gives you exposure to a wider range of people on the site. Some of the circumstances in which you may want to like a pin include the following:

- When someone has "liked" one of your pins. Take the opportunity to check out their boards and perhaps like back something they pinned.
- When you're searching the site and you spontaneously find pins that delight, amuse, or tickle your fancy.
- When you're searching pinners you follow, and you find pins that are a good fit with your brand and business content.
- When you want to save the pin for future reference. Since Pinterest keeps track of all the pins you have liked, you can find them in a flash.
- When you want to support a fellow pinner in increasing their like stats for a particular pin. Below each image, Pinterest posts the number of likes and repins that pin has received, showing the world its popularity.

By the way, you can like any pin you want on Pinterest, except your own.

HASHTAGS

If you want to ensure that a particular pin you have posted shows up when another pinner searches via a specific keyword, you can add a hashtag to that pin's description.

A hashtag begins with a # sign and is immediately followed (no spaces in between) by a word (or several words run together) that identifies it as a searchable keyword or phrase. Case doesn't count, but if your tag contains multiple words, it's easier to read if you capitalize the first letter of each one. Bear in mind that while it's overkill to hashtag every single solitary possible keyword in a board or pin description, it's important to determine which four or five keywords are the most significant to your business and brand and consistently hashmark those.

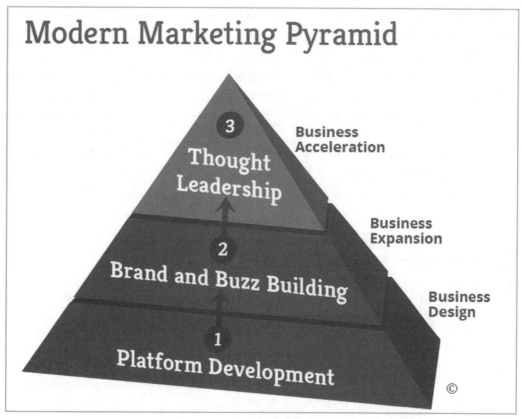

FIGURE 10–1. Use Hashtags for Keyword Phrases

For example, I posted a pin featuring the Modern Marketing Pyramid on my "Social Media Strategies" board, and put a hashtag of #SmallBusinessMarketing in the description. This way if someone on Pinterest is searching for that keyword phrase, it will show up. In addition, once you add a particular hashtag (#word) to a pin, it becomes a live link that users can click on to find other pins that have used that same hashtag (see Figure 10–1).

As you surf the site, pay attention to the keywords that other pinners in your niche are using and try to pick up on trending and popular keywords to use as hashtags.

COMMENTING

Since Pinterest does not enable members to communicate with each other privately—via direct messaging—one of the best ways to make your thoughts known is to comment on pins by clicking on the comment box that appears when you hover your cursor over a particular pin. Doing so can raise awareness about your business and brand on the site by:

- *Highlighting Your Personality.* A well-written comment that tips its hat to your style—be it funny or fact checking—is a great way to intrigue others to check you out online.
- *Spotlighting Your Site.* By commenting with some regularity on the boards that most relate to your business and areas of expertise, you can garner the attention of others in your field (and potential customers), who make good candidates for following your boards.
- *Starting a Conversation Thread.* Some pins get oodles of comments that end up in a dialog between pinners. By posting a comment that is thought-provoking, you can be the start of a conversation that creates connection between you and other pinners.

Setting Up Comment Notification

To ensure that you get notified when someone comments on one of your pins, hover over your profile picture and name in the main menu bar. A drop-down menu will appear. Click on the "Settings" drop-down and locate the "Email Settings" tab on the right and click on it. A list of email notification options will be visible. Find the one marked "Comments," and make sure it is in the "ON" position. Go to the bottom of the page and hit "Save Settings." You are now set up to receive notifications when someone comments on one of your pins (see Figure 10–2).

FIGURE 10–2. Get Set Up to Receive Comment Notification

If at first this seems like just another piece of email that will get added to the already overwhelming pile currently in your inbox, consider this: Once someone comments on your pin, or comments on your comment, you have entered into an initial dialog with them. While you have no obligation to continue the conversation, it's a smart move to go to their Pinterest profile and check it out. You may discover that it would benefit you both to know more about each other. If so, you can continue the dialog on Pinterest via a commenting thread, or even contact them through their website or other information provided in the profile.

Lastly, if you want to follow the comments others make on a particular pin (that's not one of yours), like it so that you can monitor comments as they come in.

To receive notification when someone likes, repins, or follows your pins, follow this same procedure, but locate the appropriate option and turn it to the "ON" position (see Figure 10–3).

FIGURE 10–3. Get Notified When Someone Likes, Repins, or Follows You

Types of Comments

Even if commenting on others' pins seems like a good idea, it may be less obvious what kinds of comments you can leave that will have an impact. Try these conversation starters to get the thread going:

- Agree with the pinner's point of view.

THE DOS AND DON'TS OF COMMENTING

As with other social media sites, the protocol for commenting remains the same. Do add value to the dialog by making your comments interesting, unique, funny, or insightful. Don't turn your comments into spam by self-promoting and/or linking to your own content.

Keep in mind that once you hit that little red "Comment" button, you have gone public with your point of view and anyone who views that pin will automatically see your comment placed below it. Additionally, the pinner whose pic you commented on may receive notification of your comment, depending on their settings.

Lastly, there is such thing as commenting too much, too often. While there is not a strict numerical line to avoid crossing, suffice it to say that as a general rule, if you are commenting on more than 20 to 30 percent of the pins you like or repin, you're getting near the edge.

- Disagree politely and respectfully.
- Express appreciation for the pin or board.
- Provide an interesting fact.
- Give an example.
- Ask a question.
- Tell a quick tale.

Once you have found a pin you want to comment on, and know what you want to say, the mechanics are simple. Place your mouse over the image you want to comment on, and a comment box will appear on the top right-hand side of the image. Click on the "Comment" tab, and a text box with your profile picture appears below the pin. Enter your comment and, when done, press the "Comment" button to the right, below your text.

Handle Negative Comments with Finesse

At some point in your Pinterest life, you will more than likely get a negative comment on one of your pins. If you're tempted to comment back in kind, remember that social media masters know that when it comes to handling naysayers, there are a few smart ways to deal.

Focus on Facts

If someone posts something that is factually inaccurate, you can correct it in a straightforward and unemotional way. For example, say you post a pin of a cute calico cat and get a comment pointing out that Fluffy is in fact a tabby. You can simply post a follow-up comment correcting the error, without attitude. As in, "Thanks for the comment, but the humane society where I adopted her assured me she was a calico."

Disagree Outright, but Polite

While some comments may challenge your point of view, and might even be seen as negative, they aren't overtly hostile or rude. In this case, you may want to pick up the thread of the conversation and come back with a comment as to why you disagree and restate your position with additional clarity, thoughts, or facts. The person who commented originally may not have a change of heart, but everyone else who reads the comments will at least be exposed to your point of view.

Let It Be

Not just a great Beatles song but also a viable response when an unreasonable comment has been made. There are those occasions when commenting back will only serve to further inflame the situation. In these cases, the path of least online resistance is the way to go.

Let Others Do the Talking

One of the nice things that often happens when someone makes a comment that is a) very offensive, b) seriously misinformed, or c) rude is that the community will take care of it themselves. You may not even need to comment back, since it's likely that someone else on Pinterest will come to your defense with a comment of his or her own.

If You're Wrong, Say So

Post enough stuff on Pinterest and, at some point, you will make a mistake. If someone calls you out on it, man (or woman) up and own it. Saying you're sorry and correcting the error will increase the level of trust your followers have in you.

Don't Take It Personally

Take one social network, add members, mix with comments, and hurt feelings will happen. While most of the comments you receive will roll off your back, the occasional

BLOCKING OTHER USERS

In the event that all other strategies for polite dialog fail, there is always the "Block User" feature. This feature "prevents both parties from following each other's boards and does not allow them to like, repin, or comment on each other's pins." While there is no notice that gets sent when you block someone, if they attempt to follow you or interact with one of your pins, they will discover that they have been blacklisted from your page.

To access the "Block User" feature, go to the individual profile page of the person you want to block and hover over the flag in the bottom right-hand corner of the box with their photo. A drop-down menu appears that allows you to report the person. At the very bottom is a "Block Username" option. Click on the red "Block" button, and they are out of your Pinterest life forever.

FYI, you can also report a user from the same drop-down menu for community infractions, such as pornography or hate speech. See Chapter 6 on Pinterest Etiquette for details.

bad boy will slip you up. When this happens, don't fire off a response right away. Instead, take some time to think through one of the other options above and choose the one that best fits the circumstance, not soothes your bruised ego.

TAGGING

In instances where you are following at least one board of another pinner, you can tag that person in your pin description (or comment) by inserting the @ symbol before their name. Tagging other pinners increases your Pinterest community participation and can build ties with others in your industry. Some of the reasons to tag a fellow pinner in a comment or description include:

- To recommend a pin or topic you think they would find interesting or useful
- To give them credit for content they contributed
- To let the other person know that you are aware of them
- To draw their attention to a particular pin
- To engage them in conversation and further deepen your dialog
- To promote their profile, since tags link through to the other pinner's profile
- To invite their comments and questions on a pin or topic
- To ask them a question on a pin or topic

Remember that you will receive notification when you get tagged, so make it a point to connect with that other person—who by tagging you has gone out of their way to get your attention.

To tag someone in your comment or description, type the @ symbol and, with no words or spaces in between, begin typing in the name of the person you want to tag. Pinterest will automatically start to fill in with a list of your friends whose names match. Select the name of the person you want from the drop-down menu and complete writing your comment or description.

ENGAGEMENT 2.0

Liking, hashtags, commenting, and tagging are the basic foundation of connecting with community on Pinterest. However, there are four other methods that I consider Engagement 2.0. They are:

- "Pin It to Win It" contests
- Price tags on pins
- Coupons
- QR Codes

Some would say that these are more commerce than community, but I would argue that they are a blend of community and follower building. In the online world, the lines of engagement can get a bit blurry, and as long as your boards remain informational, inspirational, and even beautiful, a small amount of commerce-type engagement never hurt anyone.

"Pin It to Win It" Contests

These are fast becoming a staple of the Pinterest community, are relatively easy to put in place, and can result in exposing your brand to a much wider audience. Here are the basics.

Create the Contest Pin

Your first task is to decide the flavor of the contest you plan on running. Some of the options include:

- Asking people to repin a particular image for the chance to enter a drawing for a prize
- Offering a prize for the best board created on a particular topic
- Holding a photo competition for the best (could be cutest, most beautiful, funniest, most creative, etc.) pin placed on one of your boards and letting your followers choose the winner
- Asking people to pin a picture of themselves using your product

Once you know what type of contest you plan to run, the next step is to design the pin and write the caption (description) that explains the action you want users to take and what they will get if they win. For example, Gifts.com (http://pinterest.com/Giftsdotcom/) created a Holiday Pinterest Board Contest offering $1,000 for the most beautiful board (see Figure 10–4 on page 116).

Make the Prize a Winner

As people repin images from your Pinterest site, or pin images from your website, you potentially get introduced to hundreds (or even thousands) of new followers.

Since the objective of these contests is to get as many repins as possible, the prize you offer should be significant. Gift certificates and cards, as well as merchandise and cash, can all be good incentives if they are seen as worthwhile by other pinners.

Have Uncomplicated and Clear Rules

The last thing you want is to be bombarded with a bunch of questions about your contest. The best way to avoid this is to keep the rules simple and straightforward. I

FIGURE 10–4. "Pin It to Win It" Contest

suggest creating a live link from the contest pin to a landing page on your website that explains the contest rules. Just remember: If you make it complicated, they won't do it. A few of the details to spell out include:

How Will the Winner Be Decided?

Will they be chosen by random, a panel of expert judges, your followers, you, an open vote, or by the number of repins accomplished?

What Exactly Do They Need to Do?

For people to participate, they have to understand what it is you want them to do. Some of the options can include:

- Pin a photo of yourself using our product.
- Pin a photo that you think best represents our brand.
- Pin a designated pin from your website.
- Create a board based on a holiday or seasonal theme.
- Create a best of _____ board.
- Create a board based on items from your online store.
- Create a board based on answering a specific question you pose.

The possibilities are endless. The important thing is to clearly state exactly what people have to do to have a chance to win. The perception that the contest is fair and relatively easy to participate in will be a key element in its success.

What Are the Prize Details?

Spell out exactly what you plan on giving away, how many people can win, whether there are any costs to the winner—such as shipping and taxes—and whether any substitutions are applicable.

What Are the Logistics of Entering?

Let users know exactly how you want them to enter the contest and what is and is not allowed. Are they going to email or tweet you the URL of the pin or board they created? Place comments on the pin itself? Use a specific hashtag or mention in their description? Etc. Lastly, what is the time frame for the contest?

PRICE TAGS ON PINS

If you have a product or service that has a set price, you can essentially put it up for sale by putting a price tag on it. To add a price, just go to the description box of the pin you want to price and type in a $ sign followed by the numerical cost.

Click the "Save Pin" button, and Pinterest will automatically add a small price sash to the upper left-hand corner of your pin. In addition, as soon as you use the price-tag feature, the pin gets populated into the Gifts section and organized by price. This means that someone may find your fine offering while surfing the Gifts section, even if they are not following your boards.

COUPONS

Pretty pins that offer savings and discounts are a good way to drive new users to your Pinterest and further engage your existing followers. You can either create a whole board dedicated to these specials or weave them judiciously into your other boards.

QR CODES

QR codes (quick response codes) are commonly aimed at mobile phone users. Users who have a camera-equipped smartphone with a QR code reader on it can scan the image of a QR code to display text or contact information, connect to a wireless network, or open a web page in their phone's browser. InterlinkOne (http://pinterest.com/interlinkone/) has a whole board titled "QR Code Examples" (see Figure 10–5).

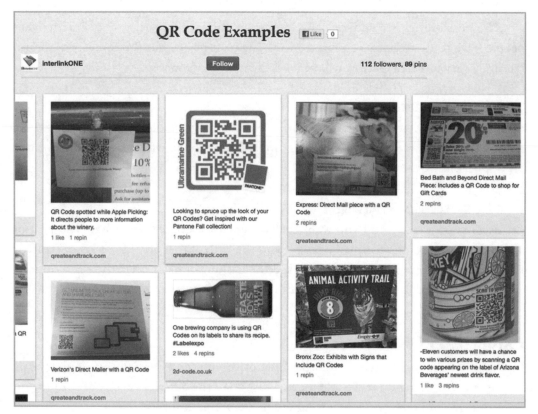

FIGURE 10–5. QR Code Examples

Some pinners are pinning QR codes as another way to drive traffic from Pinterest to their websites.

Dan Hollings, an expert on mobile marketing I interviewed for my small-business column at *The Huffington Post*, says that video is one of the most effective uses of QR codes.

"The key is to create a short video (under three minutes) about your product or service or some useful information relating to your product or service," says Hollings. "Then post the video on your website, pin it to Pinterest, and link a QR code to it. That brings the visitor to the video. It's as simple as that."

To start, check out Qr.net and createandtrack.com, just two of the hundreds of sites that offer QR code creation.

Once you've created a code, Hollings says you can then easily link it to a video, your website, or a podcast and pin it.

Well, you are off to a great start as a power player on Pinterest. If you're ready to up your game, your next move is to move from me to we and expand into collaborative pinning.

Me, You, and We:
Collaborative Pinning and Your Pinterest Strategy

While the vast majority of what you pin on your Pinterest boards will be content curated by you, there is a place for, and power to, collaborative pinning.

When you first set up a board, Pinterest gives you the option of adding the names (or email addresses) of other pinners you want to invite to participate on that particular board (see Chapter 4 for details).

In much the same way that guest blogging works, a guest pinning board involves extending an invitation to another user(s) to pin images of their choosing to a board of your designation.

Bottom line: This means you're giving other pinners admission to one or more of your boards. Whatever board(s) you invite the user(s) to pin on will feature pins of this person's choosing, promote their main Pinterest site, and, ideally, provide live links back to their website. The advantages to you of inviting a guest pinner include:

- Drawing attention to your board, since guest pinners are likely to use Twitter, Facebook, and Google+ to promote their pins to their followers on these social media sites
- Expanding the diversity of images on your board
- Reducing your content curation workload

■ Putting you in front of a wider audience, especially when the guest pinner has a large Pinterest following

There are several ways you can reach out to your fellow pinners to participate as guest pinners on one or more of your boards.

REQUEST PINS FOR A SPECIFIC PURPOSE

Let's say you're a wedding planner and have a client who's trying to decide which Hawaiian Island (Maui, the Big Island of Hawaii, Kauai, Oahu, Molokai, or Lanai) to choose as their destination wedding spot (we should all have such problems).

One creative collaboration solution would be to seek out travel experts, other wedding planners, and Hawaiian-based businesses (such as restaurants and hotels) that have a presence on Pinterest and invite them to pin their ideas.

DO A BLITZ PINNING CAMPAIGN

One option is to invite selected pinners to blitz a particular board on a specific topic for a limited period of time. For example, suppose you are an accounting firm and want to populate a board you have created called "Client Gifts Under $30." You could invite a selected group of individuals to pin to this board from the period between Halloween and Thanksgiving.

ADD GUEST PINNERS

Before you even begin to add other pinners, etiquette requires that you reach out and invite them first.

Go to the pinner's profile page and click on the world icon under their name. This will take you to their website, where you can fill out a contact form inviting them to be a guest pinner. Alternatively, you can leave a comment on one of their pins with the guest pinner request, or even email them if you have their contact information.

Once you have received the thumbs-up to grant access to one or more of your boards, click on your profile and select "Boards" from the drop-down menu. Next, click on the board you want the person to contribute to and, when it opens up, click "Edit Board" and locate the "Who can pin?" section.

ADD GUEST PINNERS, CONTINUED

Enter the name (or email address) of the pinner you want to invite. Pinterest will then offer you a list of potential matches. Select the proper persona and hit the "Invite" button on the far right. Rinse and repeat as needed until all the guest pinners you desire for a particular board have been added.

Edit Board / Personal Branding

Title	Personal Branding
Description	
Category	Education ▼
Who can pin?	Name or email address of a friend... **Invite**
	Sterling Marketing G... You created this board

Save Settings

Add Guest Pinners

HOLD A PIN PARTY

A close cousin of the Twitter party, a pin party operates on much the same following principles and practices:

- Decide on a date and time when you are going to hold the pin party.
- Create a board for the particular topic of the pin party and a hashtag that goes along with it. For example, if your pin party is going to be on ways to improve

customer service in your company, your board might be named "Improving Customer Service," and your hashtag could be #customerservice.

- Invite experts in your field or the topic to contribute pins and descriptions before the designated date and time of the pin party.
- Promote your pin party—beginning several weeks in advance—via your blog, Twitter, Facebook, LinkedIn, email list, etc.
- Invite your audience (and ask your guest pinners to invite theirs) to visit the pin party Pinterest board at a particular time and day to discuss the pins via comments.
- Do a follow-up to all your social media and your blog thanking all the guest pinners and your audience for participating.

SHARE RESOURCES, IDEAS, AND OPINIONS

Perfect for industry groups, specific professions, or individuals who have a shared passion, these types of collaboration boards build community and learning. For example, Creekside Learning (http://pinterest.com/creeksidelearn/learning-with-literature/) has a "Learning With Literature" board that has 23 guest pinners and is followed by more than 3,600 people. The board describes itself as *"full of ideas on how to learn from wonderful children's books. Crafts, projects, activities and much more based on popular children's literature with our pre-K to 4th grade kiddos."*

PROVIDE CONTENT GUIDELINES

As a starting point, only invite those people to pin whose Pinterest boards and bios you have checked out. Beyond that, providing some content guidelines will go a long way toward ensuring a successful collaboration for both you and your guest pinner. To empower your guest pinner, briefly let them know:

- Who your core audience is
- The objective for the board
- Why you asked them to pin
- What types of things you are looking for them to pin (ideas, images, feelings)
- Whether there are any types of pins you don't want
- Any promotional dos and don'ts

JOIN A BOARD

If in the course of your browsing Pinterest you run across a collaborative board you want to join, there's no harm in asking. Just go to the main profile page of the board creator and click on the world icon under their name. This will take you to their website, where you can use the contact form to make your request.

Collaborative pinning is one way of bringing your Pinterest into the fold with the rest of your social media. To get the best results, however, it pays to fully cross-publish and cross-promote your content on Pinterest to all your other social media fronts, including Twitter, Facebook, and your blog.

Pinterest on the Go:
Mobile

Pinterest offers a mobile version of the site that can be used on any touchscreen mobile device including the iPhone, iPad, and Android. Although Pinterest offers a native app for all three major players, the general consensus is that the phone apps work slightly better than the tablet ones.

NAVIGATING THE PINTEREST APP

To download the free app, go to the app store on your phone and search for "Pinterest." After downloading the appropriate app, you will be asked to log in for the first time using either Facebook, Twitter, or email. Choose one, enter your username and password, and, assuming you already have a Pinterest account, the site will recognize you as authorized and prompt you to press "OK" to continue. You are now ready to take Pinterest out for a walk.

The mobile Pinterest experience is largely similar on both the iPhone and Android apps and tablets. The tabs shown on the screen allow you to use the site much as you would from your desktop computer.

The "Following" Tab

On the far left of the menu is the "Following" tab, which is the default you see when you launch the app. The pins that appear here are the latest from the folks you follow. To see more than just the four pins immediately showing, scroll down. To view a particular pin, tap on it. An enlarged image will appear, and you will be given the option to Repin, Like, or Share it (the arrow-in-a-box icon) via a drop-down menu on Twitter, Facebook, or email. If you want to make a comment on the pin, scroll down to the comment box below. To return to the main "Following" page, tap the back arrow at the top left side of your screen.

The "Explore" Tab

Immediately to the right of the "Following" tab is the "Explore" tab, which shows the various categories of pins available. To see the entire list, scroll down until you come to the category you are interested in. Tap the arrow to the right of the category you want to view (Quotes, Sports, Home Décor, etc.), and Pinterest will "fetch" the most recent pins in that grouping. Clicking on any pin will open it up to that particular pin's page, where you can exercise the same options you have in the "Following" tab. Because the mobile version gives you a small number of pins to view at one time, this can be a less overwhelming way to search for images to repin. When done, tap the back arrow at the top left side of your screen to return to the main category menu.

In addition, the search box allows you to look for pins, boards, and people by typing in a specific term. After entering in the text of what you are looking for, be sure to tap and highlight the type ("Pins," "Boards," or "People") that fits the category you are searching for.

The "Camera" Tab

Smack dab in the middle of the menu bar is a camera icon that will allow you to take a photo (or use an existing one from your camera roll) and upload it to Pinterest on the spot. In either case, once you have taken the photo—or chosen one from your existing pics—a screen opens up where you can choose a board, describe your pin, and opt to share it on Twitter and/or Facebook—or neither. Once done, tap the "Pin It" icon, and in a few seconds your image will have made the short journey from your mobile phone to your Pinterest page. For tips on how to take the best mobile phone Pinterest pics, check out iPhone diva Lynette Sheppard's advice in Chapter 5.

The "News" Tab

To the right of the "Camera" tab is the "News" tab, which displays all the recent activity on your Pinterest profile, including who has recently repinned and liked your pins and begun following your boards. One way to take full advantage of this feature on mobile is to do a quick and easy check of who has begun following you in the past week—and, when it feels right, follow them back.

The "Profile" Tab

The tab located on the far right of the menu bar is the "Profile" tab, which opens up automatically to show your pins in chronological order, from latest at the top to oldest at the bottom. The screen also shows the number of followers you have, how many people you are following, and how many boards, pins, and likes you have. Tapping on any one of these options opens them up to a more detailed page, highlighting the specifics of that area. In other words, to see who your followers are, tap on the "Followers" box; to see who you are following, tap on the "Following" box, etc.

The "Account" Icon

Directly above your profile pic is an "Account" icon in the shape of a spoke wheel. Tapping this opens up to four options, including "Account Settings," "Pinterest Support," "Terms," and "Privacy and Logout."

The "Friends" Icon

Opposite the "Account" icon is the "Friends" icon, at the top right of the screen. Tap this icon, and a screen opens up that allows you to find friends from Facebook and/or your address book and invite them to join Pinterest.

Now that you've gotten a good general sense of how Pinterest works and can take the show on the road via your smartphone, the next major step is to fully integrate your blog and Pinterest for a powerful social media combination.

Build Your Blog with Pinterest

"If you build it, they will come." Well, that's what bloggers hope anyway. However, as any serious blogger has figured out, success is mostly a matter of writing high-quality content and then making your mark with the slow and steady work of daily and weekly marketing.

As such, bloggers are forever on the hunt for the next promotional "it" factor that will propel their posts to go viral and bring them fame and fortune. Enter Pinterest. While it may not be a panacea for post promotion, it does offer a robust path to building your blog.

PINTEREST INSPIRES CONTENT

One of the banes of a blogger's existence is the constant need to come up with fresh weekly (or daily) content that the blogger wants to write about, and that holds the interest of their audience. Pinterest can serve as an unexpected inspiration for blog post topics in at least five distinct ways.

1. Encouraging You to Think Outside the Box

Let's face it: Writing on the same topic day after day can lead bloggers into the bad habit of rehashing the same subjects, in a standard fashion, and with a similar point of view. Found images can help you move beyond what and how you normally write.

2. Surfing Pinterest for Interesting Images

Whether related to your topic or not, you are likely to stumble upon a pin (be it an idea, picture, service, product, or other) that encourages you to write a post that stretches you in some way.

3. Using Keyword Research

Because Pinterest is keyword-search friendly and utilizes such standard social media protocols as hashtags, you can easily search for and find pins associated with your blog topic.

Simply go to the search box at the top left of the Pinterest site and enter the related keyword. The resulting pins can provide you with a wealth of information about what types of blog posts you might pen.

4. Looking at Repin Rates

Consider which pins are getting repinned the most, have the most likes, and are generating the greatest amount of comments. Chances are that the pins that are most popular in a given topic are a perfect source of content for your blog.

5. Posting Photo and Video Pins

At this stage of the internet, visuals are a must-have for any blog. Stuck for a blog post one week? Why not search Pinterest and find a photo or video that your audience would appreciate and post that? Your post could be comprised of a simple introduction by you, followed by the featured photo or video pin. Courtesy, of course, requires that full credit be given to the original pinner with a link back to their board.

PINTEREST CAN DRIVE NEW READERS TO YOUR BLOG

According to a January 2012 report by Shareaholic (creators of browser, website and analytics tools), Pinterest was generating more referral traffic than Google+, YouTube, and LinkedIn combined.

By February 2012, Pinterest had surpassed Twitter as a leading source of driving website traffic. What really gives these findings their punch is that at the time of the report, Twitter (at 100 million strong) had over 10 times more followers than Pinterest (11 million).

It doesn't take too much time on Pinterest to figure out why this shift in traffic should come as no surprise. Part of Pinterest's power lies in the fact that individuals self-select the topics they are interested in.

LET PHOTOS INSPIRE YOUR POSTS AND THEN PIN

Last year I went on a trip to Vietnam and Cambodia. There I am, sitting in the great hall of the Reunification Palace, the landmark building in former Saigon where the war officially ended when the North Vietnamese crashed through its gates declaring victory.

Our tour guide—a short, slight-of-build, 20-something Vietnamese man—is explaining with great passion the history of Ho Chi Minh and the socialist party's rise to power in modern-day Vietnam.

I listen to the guide's well-rehearsed rhetoric as the bust of Ho Chi Minh looms large behind him and the blood-red, five-pointed star—the pentagram, symbol of communism—frames the bust's background. I notice he's been glancing down at something sporadically, which I assume to be his notes.

Suddenly he stops midpoint in his discourse on America's role in the war and holds up an iPad, showing the famous and moving photo of Buddhist monk Thich Quang Duc, who immolated himself. Ahh, his message may be of the socialist persuasion, but his note-taking technology was decidedly capitalist in nature. A picture is worth a thousand words, so I snapped a few pics to preserve the moment.

As I was reviewing my photos that night, I thought, "I have to find a blog post that goes with this photo." I did, and the result was a featured piece in *The Huffington Post* Small Business section titled "Enthusiasm and Entrepreneurship in Vietnam." I then pinned that photo and post to my "Social Media Strategies" board on Pinterest.

For example: Fashion, home décor, recipes, and lifestyle are some of the most popular topics on the site. Audiences visiting these pin boards have already declared themselves to be interested in that topic. In other words, they are pre-qualified as a potential customer, by interest, for your related product or service.

It makes sense that if they visit your pin board due to an interest in the topic—say, spring fashion must-haves for Fido—and you write a blog that focuses on all things dog, they are more likely to click through to your website.

CHEAT SHEET FOR BLOGGERS

A 2012 report by RJMetrics showed that the most popular categories and topics on Pinterest are:

- Home (17.2 percent)
- Arts and Crafts (12.4 percent)
- Style/Fashion (11.7 percent)
- Food (10.5 percent)
- Inspiration/Education (9.0 percent)
- Holidays/Seasonal (3.9 percent)
- Humor (2.1 percent)
- Products (2.1 percent)
- Travel (1.9 percent)
- Kids (1.8 percent)

If your blog centers around any of these topics, it's just a hop, skip, and a jump—OK, maybe only a small leap—from someone visiting your Pinterest board to reading your blog. Here's a look at a few bloggers in these various categories who are doing a great job of using Pinterest to drive traffic to their blogs.

Food Bloggers

Stephanie Manley, aka Copykat.com (http://pinterest.com/copykatrecipes/), is a popular food blogger who says that Pinterest drives more traffic to her blog than Facebook and Twitter combined. "What I love about Pinterest is that pin boards are curated by real people. Thanks to them, my website receives about 10,000 additional unique visitors a month," said Manley when she was interviewed on fellow food blogger Dianne Jacob's Will Write For Food site (http://diannej.com/blog/) (see Figure 13–1 on page 135).

In a similar fashion, top food blog How Sweet Eats (http://pinterest.com/howsweeteats/) has more than 38,000 Pinterest followers and an entire board appropriately titled "How Sweet It Is (Recipes)," dedicated to pinned recipes from her blog.

Some of the types of pins these top players post include:

- Recipes and photos of the finished dish
- Photos/video of a recipe being made
- Photos of recommended kitchen equipment
- Photos/video of a cooking technique being demonstrated
- Photos of the blogger's favorite foods at restaurants
- Photos of cookbooks the blogger loves, has reviewed, or wants to recommend

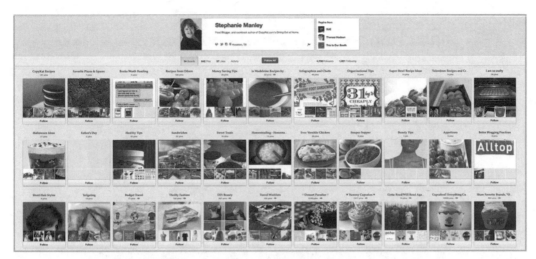

FIGURE 13–1. Copykat.com Knows Food

Beauty and Fashion Bloggers

The popular blog Crowsfeet, Cupcakes & Cellulite (http://pinterest.com/Beauty Blogger/) has taken the Pinterest marketing message to heart and has a board titled "Social Media Mentions," which features places in the media where the blog has been touted.

Some of the pins these fashion mavens place to gain traffic include:

- Photos showing the hottest fashion and beauty trends
- Photos of what's being worn by celebrities
- Photos/video of "how to" do something such as tie a scarf seven ways or make curly hair go straight

Craft Bloggers

Craft is quite simply HUGE on Pinterest and an ideal place for any craft blogger to hang out. Cindy Hopper of SkipToMyLou.org (http://pinterest.com/skiptomyloublog/) has almost 11,000 followers and 62 boards that cover everything crafty from "Knitting and Crochet" to "DIY Craft Tutorials."

It's pins like the one titled "Epsom Salt Snow"—a holiday decor pin—that make her Pinterest so accessible and popular (see Figure 13–2 on page 136).

Pins that pop for top craft bloggers on Pinterest include:

- Photos/video of seasonal craft projects—how-to or finished product with link to how-to on your website

FIGURE 13–2. DIY Snow

- Photos/video of family craft projects—how-to or finished product
- Photos/video of food- or flower-oriented craft projects—how-to or finished product

Lifestyle Bloggers

If you're on Pinterest and interested in inspirational design and lifestyle, you know blogger Joy Cho (http://pinterest.com/ohjoy/). Cho has more than 11 million followers (yes, I said million) and puts a focus on all aspects of design including a "Packaging" board, which features all manner of boxes, wrappings, bags, and bottles that house products (see Figure 13–3 on page 137).

Some of the posting strategies you can borrow from the best pinners in the lifestyle and design area include:

- Photos featuring a particular color or color palette that is being utilized in various ways for decoration
- Boards that focus on a single, narrow niche, such as Cho's "Fonts" board

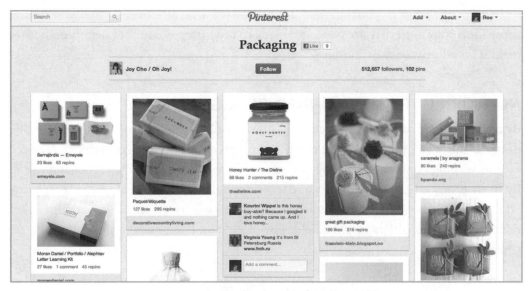

FIGURE 13–3. Packaging Makes Great Pins

EXPAND YOUR BLOG AUDIENCE BY FOLLOWING OTHER PINNERS

Much in the same way that following someone on Twitter can generate a follow back and bring you exposure to that tweeter's audience, Pinterest works in a parallel fashion.

Chances are there are other power players or online influencers on Pinterest who cater to your blog reader profile. By engaging with these hotshot pinners via liking, repinning, and commenting on their pins, you increase the chances that they will do the same for you—resulting in your pins ending up in front of your perfect audience. See Chapter 9 for details.

CREATE A BLOG THINK TANK

Who among us doesn't have a manila folder somewhere filled with pictures and postcards, pieces of paper with wise words scribbled on them, and magazine articles that inspire our creativity and stimulate our thinking?

When you create a "Blog Post Ideas and Inspirations" board, Pinterest can serve as a digital scrapbook and online think tank. Use this board as a placeholder for images, videos, quotes, etc., that you may want to blog about in the future but just don't have the room in your brain—or time on the books—to blog about right now.

You might want to consider making this board a private one, so that you can let those ideas stew until they are good and ready to be written about. For details on how to make a board private, see Chapter 4.

NETWORK WITH LIKE-MINDED BLOGGERS

By creating a pin board that is specifically aimed at gathering content from contributing pinners—other bloggers in your field—you expand your network of connections. The old idea of keeping competitors at bay has gone by the wayside in our social media world. By freely promoting other bloggers and inviting their pins, you create more interesting and diverse content for your audience, increase your outreach, and establish peer relationships with others in your field. For more details on collaborative pinning, see Chapter 11.

RESEARCH THE HOT TRENDS

Following other pinners with shared interests, using the Pinterest search bar to see what's being pinned under which keywords, paying attention to the most popular repins—all of these allow you as a blogger to see what's trending in your topic and turn it into popular posts. The more on-point your content, the more likely it is to be shared across other social media sites.

SIX BEST PRACTICES FOR BLOGGERS ON PINTEREST

Blogging in and of itself is a smoking-hot marketing strategy. Consider these statistics:

- 92 percent of companies that blogged multiple times a day acquired a customer through their blog. (HubSpot State of Inbound Marketing, 2012)
- There are 31 percent more bloggers today than there were three years ago. (eMarketer, August 2010)
- 46 percent of people read blogs more than once a day. (HubSpot Science of Blogging, 2010)
- Nearly 40 percent of U.S. companies use blogs for marketing purposes. (eMarketer, August 2010)

Given the popularity and efficacy of a blog, it only stands to reason that intelligently connecting your blog and your Pinterest boards will result in greater brand awareness and increased traffic.

1. Create Boards Based on Your Blog Categories

By mirroring some or all of the blog categories on your website as Pinterest boards, you ensure a place to pin your blog-post images and reinforce your thought leadership in those specific areas.

2. Place an Image with Every Post

By putting an image with every blog post you pen, you have the option of placing it on one of your relevant Pinterest boards—with a link back to your blog. This not only supports your link-building efforts but strengthens your brand by promoting the categories and topics you write about.

3. Put a "Pin it" Button under Each Image

Readers who are taken by an interesting image are more likely to click through and read your article. By making it easy for them to pin the specific image associated with a particular post with one click, you increase the chances that they will spontaneously do so.

4. Invite Readers to Follow You on Pinterest

Along with other social media buttons above the fold on your website, add the "P" for Pinterest. The "P," sitting side by side with the buttons for joining your LinkedIn, Facebook, and Twitter, lets visitors know that you are a serious Pinterest player and allows them to easily become a follower of your boards.

5. Place Your Blog URL in Your Pinterest Profile

Limited space notwithstanding, it's always a good idea to put the URL for your blog in your Pinterest profile. This makes it easy for would-be readers to find your words of wisdom, without having to Google you.

6. Be Consistent in Your Branding

By using the same profile picture, look, feel, message, colors, logos, and copy on your Pinterest profile as you have on your website, blog, and other social media sites, you create a congruent brand. Unless you are promoting a vastly different "you" on Pinterest than on your blog, staying consistent will strengthen your personal brand.

Regardless of your profession, knowing how to build your blog with Pinterest is an essential skill. In addition, however, many professions on Pinterest have their own unique ways of working the site to build their brands. For details, read on.

Chapter 14

Your Profession on Pinterest:
An A–Z Guide

Pinterest may be the newest player on the social media block, but its wildfire-like growth and increasing popularity mean that at some point, your customers are going to expect to find you there. Having a presence on Pinterest—as with LinkedIn, Twitter, and Facebook—is becoming a branding best practice. So, if you have not already jumped on the bandwagon, line up your images and get ready to pin.

And if you think that I'm only talking to those businesses that fall into the home décor, fashion, and food categories, think again. All manner of professions and companies—profit and social profit, startup and Fortune 500, accountants to zoos, and everything in between—are signing on.

The following is an A-Z guide of ideas on how pinners from different professions are taking advantage of the Pinterest revolution to tell the story of their brands and businesses. Even if you don't see your exact vocation on this list, or are tempted to only look at the section on your vocation, I suggest you read through the whole chapter anyway. Many of the Pinterest ideas presented here that are used by one industry can be easily adapted by another, with great results.

ACCOUNTANTS

As the official Pinterest page of The Professional Association of Small Business Accountants (http://pinterest.com/smallbizaccnts/) shows, your firm's boards don't have to be a boring barrage of tax code info. Accountants can be stereotyped as calculator-wielding nerds. Put a dynamic human element to your brand's image with boards that are a mixture of practical advice and personality.

Potential boards could include the following:

Tax Boards

A tax tips board that features stylized, short, one-sentence tax tips. Make each tip a separate pin, and place your firm's logo at the bottom to get your brand out there and promoted when your tips are repinned.

Video Tutorials

Short video tutorials that take on various tax and accounting subjects. The Institute of Public Accountants (IPA) (http://pinterest.com/ipaaccountants) in Australia has a Pinterest board called "Useful Vids," which contains original tutorials like "What Trustees Must Do for the 2012 Financial Year," and "Are You Using Accounting Information Effectively?"

Have Fun with Numbers

Taking another page from the IPA Pinterest book, they proclaim upfront in their profile, "A bit fun, a bit serious!" To this end, they have boards based on the numbers zero through nine that feature fun images related to each of the numbers. Additional fun boards include "Things Accountants Like" and "With The Money My Public Accountant Saves Me," featuring fun, aspirational luxury goods and trips (think Dubai, yachts, Rolex watches, etc.).

ACTORS AND OTHER PERFORMERS

Whether your performance art is burlesque, stand-up comedy, acting, poetry, magic, music, or any combination of the above, Pinterest can help you gain exposure for your unique creative expression.

Actress Felicia Day (http://pinterest.com/feliciaday/) is a perfect example of using the power of Pinterest to get her brand as a performer out and about. She is the creator of a video channel titled Geek & Sundry, where she features her web series called *The Guild*. Day has more than 20,000 Pinterest followers and has, among other things, a board filled with short clips from the series. If followers want to see more, they simply click the live link to *The Guild*'s official website.

A few other ideas you would-be award winners can put in place on Pinterest include the following:

Broaden Your Appeal Beyond Your Art Form

One way to get new viewers familiar with your talents is to offer a few boards that are tangentially related to your field, but of broader scope. For example, many performers carefully craft their own costumes and wear and apply their own dramatic theatrical makeup. Since makeup application (especially how-to videos) and fashion are extremely popular on Pinterest, these are great areas in which to place some of your pins.

Showcase Yourself Behind the Scenes

Use your Pinterest as a place to give your fans content that they can't find anywhere else, such as a typical day in the life of or the making of. For example, Day has pinned video production diaries that feature her and her director talking about the current season of the show. She also has a video showing a typical day on the set.

Feature Others

What performers, directors, writers, and producers would you like to work with? Be sure to do an @ mention with their names in your descriptions. Since they will be notified that you mentioned them, this increases the chances that they will see your boards, and, who knows, you could create a whole new opportunity for your career.

Demonstrate Your Diversity

Go beyond a single headshot to a board or themed boards that highlight the range of your performing abilities. Pin photos that show off different looks, styles, attitudes, instruments, and even characters that you have played.

ARCHITECTS AND INTERIOR DESIGNERS

Pinterest's focus on design and décor makes it a natural fit for architectural firms and interior designers, who inherently deal in visually rich content. A few opportunities to showcase your work, aesthetic, and ideas include:

Focus on Functional Spaces

Users are continually looking for beautiful (or clever) images of interiors to pin. Instead of lumping them all together, try segmenting them out by room or functional

FIGURE 14–1. A Focus on Foyers

space. For example, Christopher Architects (http://pinterest.com/christopherarch/) has individual boards for a study, dining room, bedroom, bath, and even foyers and closets (see Figure 14–1).

Highlight Your Specialty

If your firm has a particular area of expertise, make a point of featuring it. For example, if green architecture or design is your specialty, create a board that visualizes your philosophy of sustainability by pinning pictures of eco-friendly home products and energy-efficient designs. If your area of expertise lies in designing and decorating small spaces, create boards that show off your best examples and provide small-space interior design tips and space-saving products.

Encourage Visitors to Contribute Their Visuals

Open boards allow users to pin images of their favorite living spaces and even pictures from their own homes. A collaborative board not only helps create engagement with your audience but provides you with insight into what is resonating with potential clients.

Use Pinterest on Your iPad for Presentations

Instead of pulling out a manila file folder crammed with a jumbled mass of photographs, download the Pinterest app to your iPad and use your boards to present your best ideas. This method has the advantage of showing clients a much broader range of design options and allows you to instantly narrow down and focus on the boards that resonate the most.

ARTISTS AND PHOTOGRAPHERS

Pinterest is all about the pictures, and most artists already have an entire portfolio of pins at their disposal in the form of photographs of their work, studio, and methods—all of which make for visually rich boards.

The problem is that when Pinterest was first taking off, concerns over out-of-control copyright infringement and lack of proper credit for image sources were rampant. Fortunately, all the initial controversy has given way to a best practice where pinners have become more conscientious of proper attribution. With that stumbling block behind, if you are an artist or photographer, Pinterest is a natural fit for your professional expression.

Here are a few ways that you can use Pinterest to gain wider exposure for your work, and bring new art patrons to your doorstep:

Pin Your Portfolio

The next time you have a potential gallery or client who's interested in your work, don't just send them to your website; direct them to your Pinterest page, where they can have the full-on, dramatic impact of seeing a myriad of your images served up at a glance. In addition, be sure to offer exclusive content on Pinterest that you don't have on your website. This encourages potential buyers to go to both, and increases your exposure.

If you're hesitant because of copyright concerns, see the information in Chapter 5 on how to easily watermark your images.

Let Your Freak Flag Fly

Many artists are at their hearts truly creative and quirky types whose art expresses itself, not just on canvas or in clay, but in their lifestyle choices, including food, clothing, home décor, movies, books, etc.

Don't be afraid to let your odd, unusual, and eccentric personality out in your pin choices. That having been said, if you're a stay-at-home, introverted mom who paints beautiful pastoral landscapes—by all means, go with that.

Vanessa Johanning (http://pinterest.com/ContessaVanessa/happy-yarn/) is an example of an artist who is using Pinterest to showcase her work and her personality as a trendsetter and arbiter of cool. One unusual board called "Happy Yarn" features art made of crochet, including a telephone and a lamp cover.

Show the Tools of Your Trade

Many people are not only interested in seeing your final product but are equally as fascinated by the process you used to get there. One way to give your viewers a peek inside your artistic world is to showcase the tools you use in creating your masterpieces. For example, drawdrawdraw (http://pinterest.com/drawdrawdraw/) has more than 745,000 followers and has a super-stylish board called "Drawing Equipment," which contains pins of "stuff to draw with and on." The key here is that this pinner has framed up his photos so that pencils, chalks, and pens look sexy.

Offer Your Work for Sale

This sounds obvious, doesn't it? But many artists are missing the chance of a spontaneous sale from someone who lands on their Pinterest page and is inspired to purchase. To make it clear that a particular piece is for sale, add a price in the pin description by placing a $ sign, followed by the exact numerical cost. For example: $500 or $5.55.

Once pinned, Pinterest will automatically generate a price banner that shows up on the left-hand corner of the piece, and your item will also be added to the Gifts section on the homepage. See Chapter 10 for more details.

AUTHORS

If there is any group that can immediately benefit from participating on Pinterest, it's authors—both fiction and nonfiction. Consider these numbers from a survey by Content Connections. According to the study, the "average woman" book buyer:

- Is 45 years old
- Purchases an average of 28 books a year
- Spends $280 on nonfiction titles per year
- Makes a full third of her book purchases online
- Is more likely to visit an author's website than a publisher's website

Now line that up with some statistics pulled from Google Ad Planner that reveal that 72 percent of Pinterest users are female, and 66 percent of those are age 35 or older. See what I mean? Every author, whether self or traditionally published, has the opportunity to find an audience on Pinterest. Here's how.

Share Your Writing Life and Process

Did you write your latest novel sitting at Starbucks, tucked into a corner with your laptop, or by holing up in your apartment and eating pizza? Readers love to be let in on the small details that make up the story of how your book got written. Pin pictures and descriptions of where you write and your surrounds—empty Chinese food takeout containers and all.

Photograph Your Book Tour

Share photos from the road. It could be you at a reading, you with your fans, or the outside of the bookshop on a snowy night. You could also turn your book tour into a mini travel log of the places you've been, including photos of meals from local restaurants and pictures of quaint landmarks and cool buildings and landscapes.

Pin Your Popular Characters

Those of you who write fiction can give your characters an online life by creating boards that feature them. Include things such as where they live, what they like to eat, what they enjoy on their days off, the music they listen to, the books they read, and the clothes they wear.

Promote Other Authors

Most authors have friends who are also authors. We just seem to run in packs that way. Create a board featuring your fellow writers' published books. It helps support your community and will likely bring new users to your page. For example, Janet Evanovich (https://pinterest.com/janetevanovich/), the #1 *New York Times* bestselling author, has a board on her Pinterest simply titled "Books Worth Reading."

Another take on this is to create a board for books on a topic similar to yours. For example, if you have written a leadership book, why not pin other titles you respect in that genre? If you're worried about competition, consider this:

Chances are good that you and your fellow leadership-book author share a similar audience demographic, which means that his or her followers are likely to be interested in your book as well. Besides, have you ever known anyone who would read one book on leadership not to read two?

For more general information on writers, see "Writers" on page 158.

COACHES, CONSULTANTS, AND SPEAKERS

Life and health coaches, motivational speakers, leadership development specialists, management consultants, executive coaches, and the like can all use Pinterest to visually inspire, educate, and cultivate new and existing clients. The key is to achieve that delicate balance of providing valuable and inspiring information with just a pinch of promotion thrown in. Here's how:

Inspire with Aspirational Quotes

Quotes are one of the most popular items on Pinterest and enjoy a high repin rate. For example, Brené Brown (http://pinterest.com/brene/), the star of the runaway

TEDxHouston talk on vulnerability and author of *Daring Greatly: How the Courage to Be Vulnerable Transforms the Way We Live, Love, Parent, and Lead* (Gotham, 2012), has just such a board titled "Sparkle Plenty. Inspire Me. Twinkle." On it, Brown and her invited guest pinners have placed 206 inspirational sayings.

Pin Relevant Book Reviews

Entrepreneurs and executives consume a steady diet of how-to business books and are always on the hunt for recommendations. As part of the value you add, create a Pinterest board that focuses on reviewing and recommending business books your client base would find of use.

Tell Your Tale

Many people in the coaching/consulting/speaking world went into their profession with a sense of purpose driven by their own life experiences. Share the story of how you got into your field by pinning relevant pages from your website, videos of you speaking, and blog posts and articles you have written that enlighten your audience about who you are, why you do what you do, and the value you bring to your clients.

Make Your Pinterest a Resource Portal

Let's say you're a health coach with a specialty in weight loss. What other related resources might your clients (and potential clients) be in the market for—a fitness trainer, a stress reduction workshop, a great yoga class, or a teacher? By actively promoting resources other than yourself, and even letting them pin to your designated boards as well, you expand your value to your users, build goodwill within your network, and can even raise your visibility within your industry.

CONTRACTORS AND CONSTRUCTION COMPANIES

If you go to the Categories section on the homepage of Pinterest and click "Home Décor," you'll find everything from a DIY fire pit for sale ($30) to a tutorial on repainting and distressing old furniture. This category is one of the most popular on Pinterest and provides contractors and construction companies with an opportunity to raise their visibility with potential customers.

Pin the Transformation

Pinterest just screams out for the stock and trade of any contractor worth their salt—the before and after image. In addition to taking and pinning their own photos, contractors should encourage customers to post their pics of transformed spaces as well.

FIGURE 14–2. Tile Work

Document Your Work in Photos

In addition to before and after shots, one immediate way to create credibility is to show the quality of what you do. For example, Ceramictec Tile Contractor (http://pinterest.com/ceramictec/) in Tampa, Florida, hosts a board with pins of their tile work (see Figure 14–2).

Offer Home Tips and Product Recommendations

Boards that focus on solving a problem with products or tips—such as "How to Extend the Life of Your Marble Countertops" or "How to Clean Your Stainless Fixtures"—are always popular. In addition, you can create a top-10 list of your favorite products and techniques to handle any home situation, such as removing mold, getting gum out of carpeting, preventing water damage during a heavy rain, etc. Infographics are a great way to make how-to information more user friendly.

DANCE, THEATER, AND LIVE PERFORMANCE COMPANIES

Whether you run a theater company, performing dance studio, or symphony, you have myriad ways to use Pinterest to make your movements come alive.

Peel Back the Curtain

Give your audience a backstage look at the process that goes into creating, rehearsing, and putting on a live performance. Take a lesson from the Pittsburgh Ballet Theatre (http://pinterest.com/pghballet/) that has a "Behind the Scenes" board featuring still photos of rehearsals, as well as goings-on backstage before the show.

Ideas for pins include videos of rehearsal, images of performers doing their hair and makeup, and warming up in the wings. While you are at it, why not post an image of the snack table? Pinterest users are known to be a foodie lot, so indulge them.

Pin Your Road Trip Highlights

If your company packs up and takes the show on the road, feature pins from your travels with highlights of venues, surrounding tourist attractions, and—here comes the food theme again—fun restaurants where the company ate or bars where they had a beer, or two.

Feature Programs and Performers Past and Present

Create a board that spotlights the individuals within the company via headshots and bios, as well as playbills from all prior and current performances.

Dedicate a Board to Costumes

In addition to food, Pinterest users are big fans of fashion. Ride the sartorial wave and include preliminary sketches, the process of making the garments, and pics of the final product on stage during performance.

DOCTORS, DENTISTS, THERAPISTS, AND MEDICAL PROFESSIONALS

As of the writing of this book, there is no "Healthcare" category among Pinterest's classifications, so plan on using the "Health and Fitness" and "Education" categories for board designation. Even without the "Healthcare" label, Pinterest is a solid platform for providing patient information and support.

Throw Some Fun into the Patient Education Mix

Medical, dental, and mental health topics can be a bit heavy and scary. Balance the scales by inserting a bit of fun and lightness into your Pinterest mix. For example, Greystone OB/Gyn (http://pinterest.com/greystone3240/) has more serious pins, such as "5 Pregnancy Pains That Are Usually Harmless," alongside a "Baby Nurseries" board, which features decorating ideas and tips.

Link out to Credible Sources

It's unlikely that a dozen pins, or even a whole board, will cover all the information on a given topic, so it's essential to link out to other reliable sources of info. For example, the Greystone OB/Gyn "Pregnancy" board has pins with direct links to pregnancy.org, a site that hosts information regarding labor and delivery. If you're a Marriage, Family, Child Counselor (MFCC), you might have links out to websites with a focus on addiction, depression, and other mental health issues.

Provide Hard Data About Your Practice

The medical arena is one where your credentials will be first and foremost in a potential patient's mind. Boards that include hard information about your practice, including how long you have been practicing, certifications and degrees, areas of specialty, hospital affiliations, bios, and profiles of key staff and medical personnel are an important part of the site. Be sure to check with your attorney about any disclaimers you need to place on Pinterest to avoid having what you pin be misconstrued as medical advice.

FILMMAKERS

Joffrey Mavericks (http://pinterest.com/joffreymovie/) is a documentary film about the history of the Joffrey Ballet Company. It's been theatrically released, is available on DVD, and was featured on PBS in December 2012. Oh yeah, and the film has a whole Pinterest page devoted to it.

Joffrey Mavericks is a great example of the savvy use of Pinterest to promote a film and help it find its audience. Here are a few ideas:

Supplement the Story Told in the Film

To further engage your audience, consider pinning additional, relevant information that was not included in the film on your boards, including:

- Clips and outtakes from scenes that ended up on the cutting room floor, such as the "Video Extras from Joffrey Mavericks of American Dance" board (see Figure 14–3)

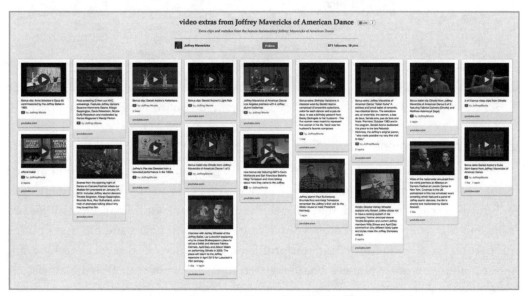

FIGURE 14–3. Outtakes from the Film *Joffrey Mavericks*

- Articles and blog posts that go into depth about some aspect of the film or story
- Interviews with the actors, director, writer, and any other persons involved in the film
- Behind-the-scenes and making-of pins (including video) are always popular with audiences who want to see how the sausage gets made, so to speak

Highlight Media Coverage

The more popular something seems, the more popular it becomes. Media coverage adds weight in the public's mind as to the value and popularity of a film. A board dedicated to the various media coverage a film receives—be it blogs, radio, TV, or print—can help create a mood of enthusiasm for the movie (see Figure 14-4).

FIGURE 14–4. The "Reviews and Media Coverage" Board for *Joffrey Mavericks*

Use Pinterest to Promote Pre-Release

One way to build up an audience for your film is to get a buzz going about it on Pinterest prior to its release. Trailers and teasers of all types can help you build up an audience just itching to see the film. A good model for this is the way book authors often push for pre-sales, months before the book comes out. Using keywords in board and pin descriptions, promoting the coming film's Pinterest profile on your other social media and blog, and guest pinning on other pinners' boards related to the topic of your film are all ways to spread the word.

LANDSCAPE ARCHITECTS AND GARDENERS

Pictures of beautiful outdoor spaces and gardens dominate the Pinscape, giving landscapers and gardeners a chance to make a name for themselves on the site.

Focus on Niche Lifestyle Boards

Addison Landscapes and Maintenance Inc. (http://pinterest.com/addisonlm/) has 27 boards, each dedicated to a different aspect of their art. For example, their board "Color of Our Moment: Green" features all things landscape- and garden-related in various shades of green. Another named "Fire Features" shows pins of outdoor fireplaces.

Make the Plants the Star

Beyond the garden-variety rose, hydrangea, and lantana bushes lies a whole world of exotic, yet practical, plants. VODA Landscape + Planning (http://pinterest.com/vodaplan/) has a colorful board titled "Plant of the Week," which features unusual plants that most people have never considered planting in their yards.

LAWYERS

Intuitively, Pinterest might not feel like an applicable social media platform for those in the law profession. However, with a little applied creativity, it might just win you over.

Highlight Your Specialty

Most practicing attorneys have an area of the law they specialize in. What's yours? For example, if you are a divorce lawyer, you might create boards that feature books on all aspects of divorce and divorce recovery, infographics featuring important divorce statistics, and the most frequently asked divorce questions.

Serve Your Community

Remember that Pinterest thrives on value, not promotion, so make sure that a few of your boards are built around bettering the community you serve. For example, Charles J. Hynes, D.A., of Kings County in Brooklyn, New York (http://pinterest.com/brooklynda/), has Pinterest boards titled "Community Initiatives," "ComALERT," and "Education and Prevention."

Pinterest and Politics

In early June 2012, First Lady Michelle Obama made headlines by activating a Pinterest account. By that point, Newt Gingrich had already been on the site for several months, Ann Romney had an active Pinterest presence, and political organizations like ThinkProgress, The Heritage Foundation, and the Democratic National Committee also had Pinterest pages.

Although Mrs. Obama was not the first political player to adopt Pinterest (her husband had one prior, but it was run entirely by his campaign), hers generated the most buzz. While the First Lady's page is mostly run by staffers, she does pin content herself and tags her pins "mo" to distinguish them from the staff-pinned content.

As politicians and their spouses are increasingly turning to Pinterest to diversify their social networking profiles, it begs the question: Is Pinterest the next big thing for politics?

Political campaigns are all about reaching out to as many people as possible, and that means it's a smart strategy to jump on the newest social media big thing, but all media are not suited to all messages. Is it possible to have valuable political conversations on Pinterest? If so, what do those look like? How do politicians and political figures use Pinterest strategically, and what is the goal of their strategy?

According to political strategists, Pinterest is not necessarily the means to attract more constituents. Rather, it can be used to foster a stronger connection with the existing base. According to various sources, Pinterest's users are 60 percent to 70 percent female. So is political outreach on Pinterest merely a "soft-sell reach-out to female voters," as suggested by Garance Franke-Ruta, a senior editor at *The Atlantic*, in her June 13, 2012, article about Mrs. Obama's Pinterest participation?

Visually oriented and light on hard facts or excessive wordiness, the nature of Pinterest makes it more suited as a platform for a personal, rather than an issue-driven, agenda.

Take Ann Romney's boards, for example. She has a board of recipes, a crafts board, and a board titled "Family" with pictures of herself, Mitt, and their kids. She also has a "Campaign" board with candid (not overly staged) pictures from the road, campaign cupcakes she created, and contests for her followers to win a lunch meeting with her or Mitt (for a campaign donation). Her boards don't exclusively focus on politics but are carefully cultivated to contribute to a positive perception of the Romney brand and to encourage interaction with followers.

Similarly, Michelle Obama's Pinterest page is highly focused on the personal. Her "Father's Day" board, for example, included a black and white photograph of Barack with their two daughters. The pin contained a link that encouraged followers to sign a Father's Day card to the President. Other pins feature pictures of Michelle with her dog, her daughters, or her garden; a picture from her wedding; etc. Michelle Obama's pins are not overtly political, but they do evoke warmth, friendliness, and a relatable ease and comfort. In short, they help reinforce positive associations around the Obama brand.

Overall, political presence on Pinterest works because visuals—when used well—can create a positive narrative about the politicians and their spouses, families, and even dogs.

Obama won his bid for re-election in 2012, but was his and the First Lady's Pinterest boards factors in generating political clout? And is it a future force for electability? That's just one of the mysteries we will have to wait and watch unfold as Pinterest matures over the next few years.

REAL ESTATE AGENTS

What better way to spotlight your listings and inspire showings than by highlighting in pictures all the big features and little details that make a property worth a visit?

As a real estate specialist, your attention to detail and attunement to the touches that make each home (or commercial property) special and unique can translate into winning pins. Here's how.

Pin Greatest Hits of a Home

While wide-angle shots of the outside of a property demonstrate curb appeal, all good realtors know that it's often one particular feature of a home that sells it. Consider dedicating a board to each property, so you can have pins that focus on the "greatest hits" highlights for each house. For example:

- Unique light fixtures
- Interesting windows or window treatments
- A customized bathroom
- A beautiful color palette throughout the house or in a particular room
- A bonus area in the house

For users who want more information, provide a URL to your site, or the dedicated site for that property, in the description. This will allow users to click through with ease. Oh, and don't forget to either take down that particular board after the house is sold or create a board called Houses Sold and feature a pin of it there.

For example, at Realtor.com (http://pinterest.com/realtordotcom/), they have a board titled "Home Theaters," which shows, among other things, a New Jersey home for sale, complete with a movie room.

Educate Your Audience

Home buying can be one of the most complicated, stressful, and confusing adult experiences. Boards that break down the home buying process step by step, and offer information on topics like first-time homebuyers, moving-in how-tos, and choosing a realtor, position you as a resource—not just a realtor.

Involve the Seller

Beyond simply showcasing the properties you have for sale, invite the seller to participate. You might create a guest board where the seller pins their favorite things about the house and surrounding neighborhood, including:

- Great things to do in the area, such as restaurants, movies, shopping, or museums
- Favorite moments of living in the house over the years
- Little positive details about the house no one else knows

RETAILERS ONLINE AND OFF

According to a 2012 Social and Mobile Commerce Study sponsored jointly by Shop.org, comScore, and The Partnering Group, U.S. consumers follow an average of 9.3 retail companies on Pinterest.

In addition, another survey from the e-commerce site Shopify analyzed data from 25,000 online stores and found that buyers who come by way of Pinterest are 10 percent more likely to purchase—and spend twice as much as those referred from Facebook and Twitter.

And finally, a Bizrate Insights survey reported that 32 percent of North American buyers bought a product after seeing it on a social site such as Pinterest.

There is no doubt that there is money to be made on Pinterest by both brick-and-mortar and online retailers. The trick is striking that delicate balance between providing value and promoting products.

One of the most followed retail brands on Pinterest is Kate Spade (http://pinterest.com/katespadeny/). While you might expect the boards on this site to be filled with the shoes, handbags, and clothing Spade showcases at her retail stores, instead the boards are a tribute to the power of color. All of Spade's boards have the name "colorfully" in them—a clear branding message as to what Spade is all about.

Another example is online retailer Holly Xerri (http://pinterest.com/HollyXerri/), creator of the Camiband multiuse wardrobe extender. Xerri ended up on Pinterest by accident. Here's her story:

"In August 2011, I went on *The Today Show* to talk about the Camiband and had what I considered to be a very successful show, resulting in 3,500 hits on our website and an influx of orders," says founder Xerri. "But in December, just a week before

Christmas, I was out to lunch with a friend when my husband kept texting me saying that we were getting a flood of orders coming in from our website. We checked our Google analytics and discovered that we had 40,000 hits to our website over a four-day period."

Xerri goes on to explain that the source of the traffic was users who had pinned her Camibands on their Pinterest pages, using images they had found on Xerri's website. "At the time, we didn't even have a Pinterest account," says Xerri.

Today, Xerri has a Pinterest presence, but she keeps the promotion low key, with only one board, "Things I Create," featuring her products. Xerri says that it's the repinning of her images that drives most of the traffic to her site, as well as the resulting sales (see Figure 14–5).

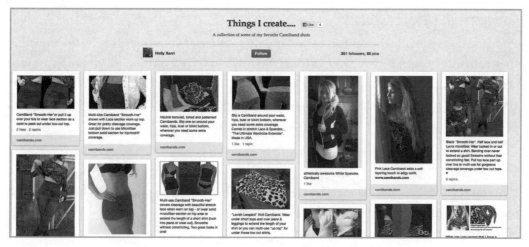

FIGURE 14–5. The Camiband: a Pinterest Hit

TEACHERS

Many educators have a love-hate relationship with social media since, with smartphones (and hence Twitter and Facebook just a click away), focus in the classroom can be compromised.

There's also the sticky issue of whether teachers should be "friends" with their students via Facebook. But Pinterest is a different beast altogether. Because it focuses on sharing visual inspiration (rather than chatting with friends), Pinterest lends itself to being a collaborative learning tool. The Convenient Teacher (http://pinterest.com/sharonl727/) teaches pre-kindergarten and has boards for both students and fellow teachers.

Use Pinterest in the Classroom

Try creating board groups aimed at increasing class participation on projects. For example, if you are doing a project in your history class about George Washington, create a board dedicated to him and that time in American history. Ask each student to find and pin an interesting fact related to the board and write a description about what they discovered.

Use Pinterest for Homeschooling

If you are a homeschool educator, Pinterest is a great way to expand your network. Consider creating a "Homeschooler" guest pinner board where like-minded educators can share curricula ideas, challenges, and homeschool solutions.

Connect with Other Educators

Pinterest does provide the option of making up to three of your boards private—meaning they can only be seen by you, and anyone you invite to pin. To this end, you may want to create a professional board where you and your fellow teachers can pin and discuss more serious topics like behavior management in the classroom and dealing with stressed parents—issues that your fellow teachers will understand all too well.

Go Juice Box

Pinterest boards can also be used by teachers for fun. Boards dedicated to healthy snack ideas, great classroom crafts for holidays, seasonal lesson plans, and fun science projects all make great pins.

WRITERS

As any writer will tell you, a good deal of our time is spent in a room by ourselves, hunched over a keyboard, typing away like a crazy person.

Pinterest can be an invaluable way for writers to break out of the natural isolation of the profession and connect with their fellow scribes and readers.

Lend a Helping Hand

While writing is an art, breaking into getting published is just as much a science. Boards that help your fellow writers (and would-be writers) understand the business of writing are always popular.

Writer's Relief (http://pinterest.com/writersrelief/) is an author's submission service that states their mission as "helping creative writers get published by targeting their

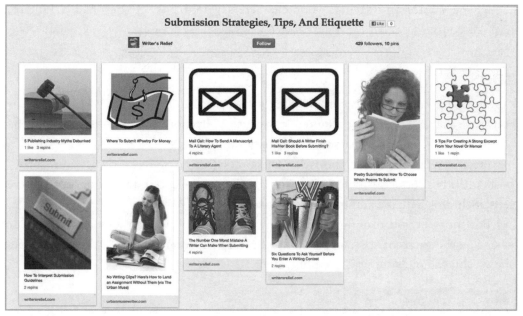

FIGURE 14–6. How to Submit Your Writing for Publication

poems, essays, short stories, and books to the best suited literary journals and agencies." Their boards offer advice on all aspects of writing and publishing, including a board on "Submission Strategies, Tips, And Etiquette" (see Figure 14–6).

If you want to find fellow writers, click on the "Followers" tab on the Writer's Relief Pinterest page and a whole page of their fans will pop up. Do some research, and pick and choose who you might want to reach out and connect with.

Ask for Help to Get over a Hump

Stuck on finding a visual metaphor you need for your story, a name for your main character, or a tidy title for your new novel? Pose a pin for discussion, asking fellow pinners to pin their solutions and suggestions to a guest board you have created for just that purpose.

Storyboard Your Characters

If you've got a case of writer's block and are feeling stuck in your story, surf the site and see what visuals inspire you. Then use the board or boards as a placeholder for ideas to develop and draw on, including a board for:

- The physical look for your story's characters: hair, fashion, makeup.
- The interior and exterior surroundings where your characters live.

■ The quotes and sayings your characters would post if they had a Pinterest account.

ZOOS

Admit it: You knew this was coming, didn't you? It's the only real Z, and besides, many zoos have a strong presence on Pinterest because really, nothing makes a better pin that some cute and cuddly—or fearsome and feisty—animal.

For example, the world-famous San Diego Zoo (http://pinterest.com/sandiegozoo/) posts include a "Squeee!" board featuring just about the cutest animal photos I've ever seen, including a mama and baby giraffe kissing.

For those of you reading this who are currently in between jobs and wondering when you will get a chance to apply all these great ideas, don't worry. As the next chapter shows, you can pin your way to employment.

Pin Your Way to New Work:
Job Hunting and Client Acquisition

Pinterest is more than just a social media phenom used by businesses to enhance their brand. It can also be a boon to job seekers and freelancers looking to build a client base or find employment. Some companies are even using Pinterest to promote and post jobs.

By building a visual resume on Pinterest—a place to send, and be found by, potential employers and clients—you can pin your way to new work. Here's how:

CREATE A RESUME OR PORTFOLIO BOARD

Begin by adding a new board to your account that is dedicated to showcasing your work, career achievements, and professional accomplishments. Using the word "Resume" or "Portfolio" in the board title, along with your name or job title, ensures that potential employers and clients will know what they are looking at. Don't forget to add a brief description to your board that states what your work objectives are, the types of clients (or companies) you are looking to connect with, and where you can be contacted.

In addition, think about what keywords a potential employer might be using to find you. For example what words or phrases represent the job titles, qualifications, skills and abilities an employer would search for? For more details on where to find keywords, check out Chapter 4.

MAKE A MOCK JOB INTERVIEW VIDEO

Media coach and sound bite expert Susan Harrow (http://pinterest.com/susanharrow/) suggests making and then pinning a video of yourself doing a mock job interview for potential employers.

Ask and Answer Three Typical Questions

The goal of the video is to cover the three typical questions an interviewer might ask, and then answer them. You can use an off-site interviewer to pose the questions or simply put each question up on the screen before responding. Here are Harrow's top three questions and answers:

1. Describe a difficult situation you encountered at work that was hard to resolve: How did you handle it? "Employers want to see exactly how you deal with adversity," says Harrow. "So in some way, shape, or form, you will always get that question in a job interview." When responding on the tape, be sure to:

   ■ Briefly describe the circumstances that made the situation difficult.

   ■ Explain exactly what actions you took (what you did and did not do) in the situation.

   ■ Outline how it was resolved in the end (positive or negative) and what your part was in the resolution—even if it was a team problem. What did you contribute?

   ■ Discuss what you learned from the situation and how you grew from it.

   ■ Expand on how would you handle a similar situation going forward in your career.

2. Describe one of your greatest life or career achievements: Why is that important to you? "You need to think about the qualities, skills, and knowledge that the types of companies you want to work for desire," says Harrow. "Figure those out, and then, using a real and authentic example from your life, craft your response around them."

3. What was a situation where you had to handle a difficult person on the job? A cousin of the difficult situation problem, this question demonstrates your ability to deal with difficult people. For example:

   ■ A strong disagreement took place on your team, and one of the members was unwilling to listen to other points of view.

MAKE YOUR INTERVIEW ANSWERS AS RESULTS-BASED AS POSSIBLE

When it comes to crafting our words, we writers have a saying: "Show, don't tell." In much the same way, Harrow suggests that the answers to all the questions in the mock interview video need to demonstrate clearly the results you have produced. Let's say you wanted to show that you have great research skills. Instead of simply stating on the tape, "I have great research skills," you would describe the specifics of a situation that show these in action.

For example, suppose you had a situation in which your company asked you to produce a last-minute research report—in a day. You might discuss not only how you produced it in half a day but also describe all the additional information you added to the report that was not part of the original request. This shows your research abilities, rather than just stating them.

- You had a customer who called you up ranting and raving about an inaccurate order.
- You worked for a boss who took your ideas and represented them as his or her own.

The story you choose to tell should involve having to work with someone who is obviously demonstrating a negative emotion or characteristic, such as fear, anger, selfishness, stubbornness, etc. Harrow suggests having your answers follow the Situation, Action, Results pattern.

- *The Situation.* Explain what the situation was and the specific behaviors and attitudes expressed by the other person involved. Stay away from labels (i.e., "He was a real jerk") and instead focus on tangibles, such as, "He came into my office yelling and pounding his fist on my desk, demanding an explanation for the inaccurate invoice."
- *The Actions.* Describe the actions you took to deal with the person. What did you actually say and do? "The key here is lively details," says Harrow. For example, instead of saying, "I calmed him down," paint a picture of your behaviors by saying, "I didn't interrupt him with my point of view when he first started venting but instead nodded occasionally and told him I understood his frustration. Then I invited him to have a seat, offered him a cup of coffee or tea, and asked him to take me through the situation step by step so we could resolve it."

- *The Results.* After all was said and done, what were the results of the strategy you chose to employ with this person? Again, try and stay away from generalities, such as, "They calmed down," and focus on outcomes, such as, "They apologized for getting so hot under the collar, and we mutually agreed upon a plan for moving forward."

Best Practices for Mock Video Interviews

The best videos are those that move quickly, focus on specifics, and communicate the interviewee's substance and style. Among Harrow's recommendations:

- *Think TV News Segments.* Harrow says that the videos need not be long in length but more like TV news segments. She suggests putting together either one four-minute video, where you move briskly through the questions, or making three two-minute videos, focusing on one question each.
- *Focus on Benefit to the Company.* Whenever possible, try to demonstrate how your actions had a bottom-line impact on the company. "Having the necessary skills is only one part of the equation," says Harrow. "You need to show how you will contribute to the overall success of the company and be someone a possible employer can see fitting into the company culture."
- *Let Yourself Shine Through.* "You are not just competing on your skill set," says Harrow, "but on who you are." If an employer is looking at two possible candidates' resumes on Pinterest and both have equal skill sets, the one who shows more of their personality and style via video may have the edge.

While most traditional video resumes are of the talking-head variety, occasionally someone breaks out of the box and gets creative, truly showing their style and flair. Take this pin from Joshua Waldman (http://pinterest.com/joshuawaldman/). He posted a resume video from Torrey Taralli, who sent it to Carrot Creative in an attempt to entice them to hire him. The catch? The stop-motion video took more than 300 carrots (yes, the vegetable) to produce and 12 hours of work.

Use Sound Bites to Get the Message Across

Harrow says that planning out and planting a few one-liners or short sound bites is a great way to be memorable. Some good sound bites to focus on include:

- Any statistics, numbers, or quantifiable results you can quote that show how your skills can be measured in real-time results.
- Stories that show the "happiness factor." Short tales that demonstrate how your participation in a situation led to greater satisfaction, teamwork, engagement, morale, and other desirable company culture conditions.

■ Details that show the scope of your work. Why is what you have done impressive? For example, instead of saying, "I've worked all over the world," say, "I've worked in over 50 different countries."

Craft the Questions First and the Answers Second

"The point of this video is to show the employer that you are the one," says Harrow. She suggests figuring out what's most impressive in your background and then determining the exact way to word each of the three core questions to show off your skills and talents.

CONNECT WITH COMPANIES AND CLIENTS YOU WANT TO WORK FOR

If you have a particular company or client in mind you want to work for, do some research on them by checking out their Pinterest boards and following, repinning, commenting on, and liking some of their pins. They will be notified of the actions you took, and you will gain some insight into how you might be a good fit and can then pin accordingly. If you end up getting an interview, be sure and mention a pin or two you saw on their page.

Even if the company does not have a Pinterest presence, you can get on their radar by pinning content from their website and/or blog and then posting it to your Twitter and Facebook accounts.

PLAN OUT YOUR PINS

Since this board is specifically designed to attract and engage potential employers and clients, you want to think through and strategize the pins you post. Some of the types of pins you may want to consider given your objectives include:

■ Relevant jobs you have held
■ Noteworthy projects you have participated in
■ Your education and degrees
■ Blog posts, articles, or other writing you have done
■ Testimonials from former employers or clients
■ Other social networks, such as LinkedIn
■ Your full resume
■ Awards you have won
■ Samples of your work
■ Press coverage on you or your work, including articles and radio and TV interviews

PIN WITH PANACHE

This is your opportunity to step outside the stuffy box of boring and add some jazz to what you post. Consider how you might characterize your career in images—and then get creative. For example, digital strategy consultant Michelle Magoffin (http://pinterest.com/peevedmichelle/) pinned a colorful and information-filled infographic-style resume that highlighted her experience, results, and creativity (see Figure 15–1 on page 167).

If you're inspired by this, scads of ideas on how to make your resume come alive on the Pinterest page can be found at http://pinterest.com/source/mostcreativeresumes.com/.

Apart from pinning a compelling resume, you can look to your profession itself for ideas to pin on your portfolio board. For example:

- *Interior Designer.* Post before and after photos of rooms you have renovated for clients.
- *Makeup Artist/Hairdresser.* Pin pics from brides and other special occasion jobs you have worked on.
- *Salesperson.* Put up a PowerPoint or SlideShare presentation that you did for a previous job.
- *Consultant or Coach.* Do you have a video of yourself giving a presentation? A short testimonial from a client? A bold statistic of something you achieved? If so, post it.
- *Web Designer.* Show off screen shots of your best homepage designs.
- *Freelance Writer.* Pick and post a dramatic photo that relates to articles, blog posts, books, and any other writing you have done, and then link it to that work. If you

RESEARCH YOUR CAREER CHOICES

If you're in the market for a job, but just not sure in which field your next vocation will fall, Pinterest is a great place to begin. Browse the categories to see which areas catch your eye or search the boards in a field you're already interested in. For example: If you think you might be up for pursuing a job as a pastry chef, you can search the topic on Pinterest and spend the next hour (or week) perusing all the luscious goodies you could create as part of your next career.

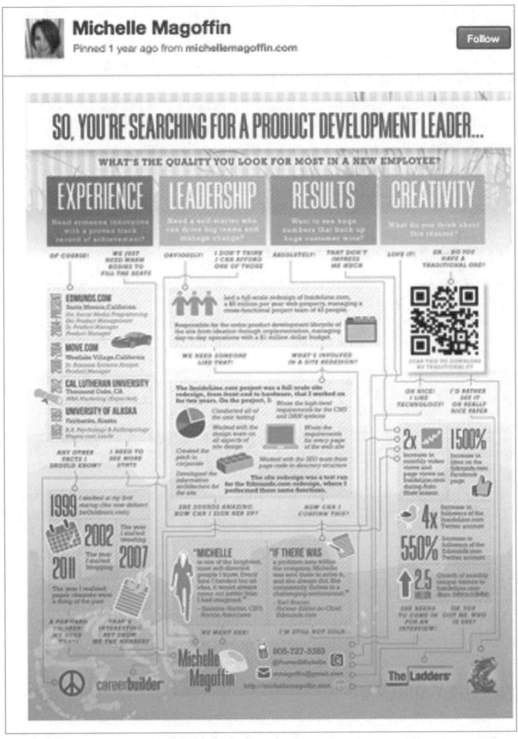

FIGURE 15–1. Creative Resume

have written for major publications, pin an image of that magazine or newspaper, with a link to the article online.

MAXIMIZE YOUR DESCRIPTIONS

Don't forget to add to each pin a description containing links to relevant web pages. In addition, use keywords that potential employers or clients might use to increase the chances they will find you when they do a search. Lastly, be sure to highlight not only what you did but any tangible results you produced. Did you save the client money? Get the job done ahead of schedule? Increase sales by a certain amount? Anything you can do to quantify your value to a potential employer or client increases your worth.

KEEP UP WITH CAREER EXPERTS

A whole slew of career-centric coaches, university departments, websites, and employment experts have made their presence known on Pinterest. For example: the Pinterest board at FlexJobs (http://pinterest.com/flexjobs/) provides oodles of info on all things job-hunting related (see Figure 15–2).

FIGURE 15–2. FlexJobs Has All Things Job-Hunting Related

In addition, CareerBuilder's board http://pinterest.com/source/careerbuilder.com/ highlights economy and job-oriented data.

PUT THE WORD OUT

Once your portfolio/resume board is up and running, it's time to spread the word. Find the dedicated URL for that board and go wide by sharing it on your other social networking sites. You might even want to print the link to your Pinterest portfolio on your business card. Consider this: Your Pinterest resume can function as a "mini-website," where you can direct potential clients and employers to discover at a glance who you are and what you offer.

Well, I take my hat off to you. You have now learned just about all there is to know about doing business with Pinterest. There's just a short ways to go, but first, you need to figure out how to measure the results you are getting from all this work you are doing on Pinterest.

Track Your Pinterest Performance

Congratulations. You have made it almost to the end of this book, and I am assuming that at this point, you are an old pro at the ins and outs of pinning to build your brand and business. There's only one thing left to do: Measure the results of your pinning efforts.

Like all social media strategies, using Pinterest requires constant monitoring and pivoting to produce the best results possible. To that end, here are some useful tools for tracking your Pinterest performance.

THE ACTIVITY TRACKER ON PINTEREST

As a starting point, you can always see the up-to-date number of followers you have on your main Pinterest page by viewing the bar directly below your profile photo. Likewise, when you click on one of your individual pins, the information at the bottom, under the image, shows how many repins a particular pin has enjoyed.

It's important to keep track of even these basic results, since they can provide tremendous marketing insight and inform adjustments you may want to make in your overall pinning strategy.

PINTEREST.COM/SOURCE/YOURURL

If you want to see what other people are pinning from your website, enter the above URL and put the name of your website into the space where it says "yourURL." For example, if I wanted to check on what images were being pinned from my website, I would enter pinterest.com/source/karenleland.com.

GOOGLE ANALYTICS

Google Analytics (http://www.google.com/analytics/) is a great tool for identifying the amount of traffic you are getting on your website and from what sources, including Pinterest. Google Analytics also offers an "e-commerce" tab to track the sales that come from particular sources. Free and easy to use, Google Analytics provides you with a detailed understanding of what is and isn't working in your pinning strategy to drive traffic and sales to your site.

PINREACH

This tool calculates a score based on a combination of your Pinterest activity, including pins, repins, likes, followers, etc. The makers of PinReach have not revealed exactly how the score is calculated, but someone else repinning your content is more valuable to your score than your own pinning activity. Having larger numbers of followers also increases your score, as does following more people (though not as much as being followed). Scores range from 0 to 100. Interestingly, the higher your score, the more difficult it becomes to raise it.

To sign up for PinReach, go to http://www.pinreach.com/auth/register and enter your Pinterest username, your email address, and a new, PinReach-specific password (not your Pinterest password).

Once you have created your account, your homepage will feature a series of graphs detailing your score history, popular pin history, and popular board history. Click the "Boards" tab at the top of the page, and you can find your board rankings (repins, followers, pins, likes, and comments). On the right side of the screen, there is a small chart detailing the basics of your entire Pinterest account, including your PinReach score. The detail offered by PinReach provides you with an in-depth understanding of what type of content your followers find hot, and not.

CURALATE

Curalate specializes in "social curation" that focuses specifically on the images being shared on Pinterest. Its service uses image-recognition algorithms to monitor your brand's social media influence. Curalate boasts that they can provide the most comprehensive understanding of a brand's social curation presence, allowing a brand to "listen in" to the Pinterest conversation that is going on around their brand. Curalate charges for its services, but you can sign up for a free trial at www.curalate.com.

REACHLI

Formerly known as Pinerly, the analytics tool Reachli is a popular service for creating and managing targeted Pinterest (and other social media) campaigns. With the Reachli interface, you are able to track and analyze metrics and clicks, enabling you to get a better understanding of your audience.

Reachli is aimed at two types of users: content creators, referred to as "publishers," and companies or brands looking to promote their products effectively online, which Reachli calls "advertisers."

If you are an advertiser, Reachli will help you distribute visual content across the web, both to social media (including Pinterest, Tumblr, Google+, and Twitter) and in the form of a lifestyle ad. Reachli uses "pair and match" algorithms to determine the most natural online locations for your content.

To create a campaign, you must first upload visual content to the Reachli interface and click the "Campaigns" button at the top of your home screen. You will then be instructed to upload a new image, either from a specific URL or by selecting a file from your computer. Once you have chosen the content, you add a description and a URL.

The "Analytics" button at the top of your home screen allows you to measure the effectiveness of your campaigns over time, in graph form. Effectiveness is measured by clicks, likes, repins, and reach.

Reachli also offers quick tips on how to pin/create content more effectively, which can be very helpful for beginning pinners. Located on the right side of the screen, the tips are made to look like Post-It® notes.

Chapter 17

In Conclusion:
Your Parting Party Gifts, and What's Next?

E very journey must come to an end, and ours has. Except—not really. We all know that education and information are a first step, but it's the consistent, steady, and small actions that we take, over time, that count.

To that end, I've a few things to share with you, including several supplemental materials to offer via my website, some suggested ways we can stay in touch as your next steps in using Pinterest for your business unfold and evolve, and a specific process you can follow to implement the ideas in this book.

CLAIM YOUR PINTEREST PARTY GIFTS ONLINE

As a thank you for buying this book, please log in to my website at www.karenleland.com to pick up your parting party gifts. These complimentary materials are designed to supplement the information in this book and include:

- A bonus chapter available only on my website as an ebook—"Chapter 18: Pinterest in 15 Minutes"—about social media time management.
- A cheat sheet of 50 ways to use Pinterest to promote your business and build your brand.

- A podcast interview with me, where I highlight your top five opportunities on Pinterest and the top five biggest Pinterest mistakes businesses make.
- A short screencast webinar on using Pinterest for business.
- A free quiz to find out where you are overall in Modern Marketing for your business.

PLEASE STAY IN TOUCH

I'm always interested in hearing from my readers, and I often feature them and their businesses in my blog posts and books, the articles I write for magazines and newspapers, and in my featured small-business blog on *The Huffington Post*. So, if you are so inspired or inclined, please use the contact form at www.karenleland.com and share:

- New tips, tools, and techniques you have learned for using Pinterest for business
- Ways in which this book has helped you expand your business and brand
- Your Pinterest success stories
- Content you would like to see included in future editions of this book
- Questions you have about using Pinterest for business

CONNECT WITH ME ON SOCIAL MEDIA

What kind of branding and marketing consultant would I be if I didn't provide my social media contacts and invite you to play with me? That said, please connect with me so that we can continue the social media conversation at:

- Twitter: twitter.com/Karenleland
- LinkedIn: Linkedin.com/in/karenleland
- Pinterest: Pinterest.com/karenleland
- Facebook: Facebook.com/sterlingmrktggroup
- The Modern Marketing Blog: www.karenleland.com/blog

PIN THIS BOOK!

If you like this book and found it worthwhile, I would of course love it if you would pin it! Book images for pinning are available on my website at www.karenleland.com.

RENT MY BRAIN©

Need a fresh perspective on your brand? Desire an action plan for Pinterest? Need expert advice on moving your business, brand, and social media to the next level?

Rent My Brain© is my one-hour, no-holds-barred consulting call that gets to the heart of your marketing, social media, PR, branding, business development, or content/internet marketing question.

The feedback you will get is to the point and precise and comes from my 25 years of experience as a marketing and management consultant, bestselling author, worldwide keynote speaker, and freelance journalist. You will leave the call with a doable action plan that you can immediately put into place. For inquiries or to schedule, go to www.karenleland.com/consulting/lightning-strike-strategy-session/.

HIRE ME TO SPEAK AT YOUR NEXT CONFERENCE OR MEETING

If you think your group, team, or association could benefit from a keynote speech, off-site strategy session, or short (yet tip-packed) talk on Pinterest (or on marketing/branding in general), please give me a shout-out at www.karenleland.com. You can also download a one-sheet list of my speaking topics at: www.karenleland.com/speaking/marketing-keynote-speaker/.

A THREE-STEP PROCESS TO IMPLEMENT WHAT YOU HAVE LEARNED

I've taught and written about time management and productivity for more than 25 years, and if there is one thing I'm absolutely convinced is true, it's that slow and steady wins the race.

This book came at you at a million miles an hour with ideas, tips, case studies, and examples that no doubt generated a huge Pinterest "to do" list—either in your head or on paper.

In my experience, it's often the case that, despite our best intentions, that social media "to do" list can become overwhelming and lead to a deer-in-the-headlights paralysis, where we do much more thinking about doing than actual doing. To prevent that from happening to you, and to actually implement the ideas in this book, here are a few simple steps to follow.

Make a "To Do" List

Based on the actions you want to take after reading this book, create an actual Pinterest "to do" list, and divide that list into three categories:

1. *Basic, must-do Pinterest items*. These are the essentials for getting your Pinterest up and running and in good shape for your followers.

2. *Brand-building Pinterest items.* These are the actions on Pinterest that will proactively help you to expand your brand and business.

3. *Breakthrough Pinterest items.* These are those projects you want to do associated with Pinterest that would be a major undertaking. They more than likely would take time and cost money, but would have a big payoff.

The trick is to start with the basic must-dos, move on to the brand-building, and then take on the breakthrough items.

Time Block

To make the time to do the above "to do" list, you are going to need to either hire some help or clear some space on your calendar to do the work yourself.

A simple and proven method for making the time to get something done in a focused way is time blocking. This is where you take a specific date and time in your calendar of anywhere from 15 minutes to an hour and block it off to focus on one specific task, and one task only—in this case, your Pinterest "to do" list.

These time blocks involve:

- Turning off your email
- Turning off your cell phone
- Letting your co-workers know you are going into a "do not disturb" space

When your time block session begins, it's helpful to set a timer so that you know when the blocked time period is up.

As simple as this sounds, it works. How do you think I wrote a 50,000-plus-word book on Pinterest and kept up a full consulting client load?

Go for Progress, Not Perfection

One of the biggest breakdowns I see my clients struggle with when it comes to marketing is their desire to get it perfect before they launch. Well, it's never going to be perfect, and if you wait until it is, it won't be at all.

With regard to your Pinterest "to-do" list, decide ahead of time what "good enough" would look like, and go for that. I'm not suggesting that you settle for mediocrity; I am suggesting that you launch reasonably well, and then improve over time.

Phew! You made it. With this last piece of the puzzle done, you can put your Pinterest strategy in place and test and improve it until you're satisfied that it's working for you the way you want it to. I, for one, am expecting great things from you. Now go out there and pin me proud.

About the Author

Karen Leland is the President of Sterling Marketing Group, where she does branding and marketing strategy and implementation. Through her unique business processes, *The Modern Marketing Pyramid©, The Brand Mapping Process©,* and *The Buzz, Buzz, Boom Marketing System©,* she helps businesses leverage new and traditional media to build stronger brands, expand their audiences, and become thought-leaders in their fields.

In addition, Karen works with startup founders, high-end entrepreneurs, and Fortune 1000 executives in the United States, Europe, and Asia to develop leadership presence through personal branding, team branding, and high-performance productivity. Her clients include: AT&T, Apple, American Express, Cisco, Johnson & Johnson, Marriott Hotels, Oracle, and Twitter.

She is the bestselling author of seven books, which have sold more than 350,000 copies and have been translated into ten languages. Karen is a sought-after speaker and has keynoted for hundreds of conferences and associations including The Young Presidents' Organization, The American Management Association, and The Direct Marketing Association. She has been interviewed by *The New York Times, Fortune, Inc., Oprah, The Today Show,* CNN, and *The Wall Street Journal.*

As a freelance journalist, Karen has written articles for *Self, Woman's Day, Entrepreneur, The Los Angeles Times,* and others. She writes a regular business blog for *The Huffington Post* and *PsychologyToday.com.*

In addition to her work in the business world, Karen has worked as an actress and has experience doing industrial films and voiceovers as well as performances on stages throughout the Bay Area and Los Angeles. She is also an exhibiting mixed media artist whose work has been shown in the Museum of Fine Arts in Boston and the Triton Museum of Art in Santa Clara, as well as other venues.

She lives in Marin County, California, with her husband, Jon.

To book a Rent My Brain© consulting session, hire Karen to keynote at your next conference, inquire about her branding and marketing consulting services, or download additional free tips, ideas, ebooks, webinars, and other goodies on Pinterest and other social media and marketing topics, please visit www.karenleland.com.

Index